An Introduction to Dyslexia
for Parents and Professionals

of related interest

Dyslexia and Alternative Therapies
Maria Chivers
ISBN 1 84310 378 8

Surviving the Special Educational Needs System
How to be a "Velvet Bulldozer"
Sandy Row
ISBN 1 84310 262 5

Dyslexia
How Would I Cope?
3rd edition
Michael Ryden
ISBN 1 85302 385 X

Practical Strategies for Living with Dyslexia
Maria Chivers
ISBN 1 85302 905 X

"Many parents and teachers are perplexed by the phenomenon of an otherwise capable child who struggles to learn to read and spell. This contemporary, practical book is an invaluable introductory resource for parents and teachers who wish to increase their understanding of dyslexia. Several chapters delve into the essential characteristics and subtypes of this disorder with clear explanations of how reading disorders affect academic, emotional, and social functioning. This book truly provides comprehensible answers to a complex lifelong disorder. The overall conclusion that emerges is that dyslexia is treatable, but can result in lifelong challenges. These obstacles can be mitigated through self understanding, as well as support and empathy from knowledgeable teachers and parents who provide appropriate interventions and accommodations."

– Nancy Mather, Ph.D.
Professor of Learning Disabilities, University of Arizona

An Introduction to Dyslexia for Parents and Professionals

Alan M. Hultquist

Jessica Kingsley Publishers
London and Philadelphia

First published in 2006
by Jessica Kingsley Publishers
116 Pentonville Road
London N1 9JB, UK
and
400 Market Street, Suite 400
Philadelphia, PA 19106, USA

www.jkp.com

Library of Congress Cataloging in Publication Data

Hultquist, Alan M.
    An introduction to dyslexia for parents and professionals / Alan M. Hultquist.
      p. cm.
    Includes bibliographical references and index.
    ISBN-13: 978-1-84310-833-7 (pbk. : alk. paper)
    ISBN-10: 1-84310-833-X (pbk. : alk. paper) 1. Dyslexia. 2. Learning disabilities. I. Title.
    RJ496.A5H85 2006
    618.92'8553--dc22

                                    2006004147

British Library Cataloguing in Publication Data

A CIP catalogue record for this book is available from the British Library

ISBN-13: 978 1 84310 833 7
ISBN-10: 1 84310 833 X

Printed and bound in Great Britain by
Athenaeum Press, Gateshead, Tyne and Wear

This book is dedicated to my parents,
Alma B. (Ekstrom) and Everett A. Hultquist

Reading levels

Throughout this book US grades are used to describe reading levels.

US grade	Typical age range
Grade 1	6 to 7
Grade 2	7 to 8
Grade 3	8 to 9
Grade 4	9 to 10
Grade 5	10 to 11
Grade 6	11 to 12

CONTENTS

CONTENTS

ACKNOWLEDGMENTS

I would like to thank Sharmon Simoneau, Paul Donahue, PhD, Robin Stander, and Kathy Johnson for their input into early drafts of this book. The international information would not have been possible without the help of numerous people from around the world who were kind enough to respond to my emails. These include Rosie Bissett at the Dyslexia Association of Ireland, James Chapman at Massey University in New Zealand, Sharon Duncan at Dyslexia Scotland, James Foster at SPELD New Zealand, Elaine Miles and Rhiannon Rowlands at the Dyslexia Unit of the University of Wales in Bangor, Louise Ward at the Canadian Dyslexia Association, Lynda Werda at SPELD Queensland (Australia), Carol Youngs and an anonymous person at the British Dyslexia Association, and a kind soul from the Dyslexia-SPELD Foundation of Western Australia who would rather remain anonymous. I hope I have not forgotten anyone. I am, of course, also grateful to the editors at Jessica Kingsley Publishers.

I am indebted to Lorna Murphy, EdD for the advice she provided. Lorna read this manuscript many times during its evolution, but her involvement goes back even further. She was a guiding force in my doctoral studies and the instructor who made being in debt worthwhile. I consider myself extremely fortunate to have had the chance to study under her expertise.

It goes without saying, but this book also would not have been possible without the support of my husband, Brendan.

Finally, despite the help and guidance of numerous people, this book is my own work and errors (with the obvious exception of things beyond my control) are my responsibility.

PREFACE

dys = difficulty

lexia = words

A quick search on Amazon.com produced over 470 publications with the word *dyslexia* in the title. Undoubtedly, some of these are out of print, but the quantity of books still raises the question, "Why do we need another book about reading disabilities?" Perhaps the best way to answer this is to state what my goals were in writing this book. In short, I wanted to write an accessible, practical, and up-to-date introductory book for parents. I wanted a book that parents could sit down with after a day of work, chores, errands, and children and read a chapter or two of without having to devote a lot of time to it and without needing a college degree in reading psychology. Unfortunately, regardless of how easy to read I tried to make this book, it was impossible to avoid using professional terms. Therefore, some words that parents may not be familiar with are printed in italics the first time they appear in the book. These words are defined in the glossary.

My experience has been that parents are initially looking for understandable answers to the most basic questions. Once the basics are there, a foundation is present for them to build on with further readings. Surprisingly, it is not only parents who often need this information. Educators (even special educators) do not always know much about dyslexia, although it is the most common type of learning disability.

In addition to being understandable, this book is also intended to be practical. For example, I wanted to offer parents an introduction to the types of things either they can do to help their children with dyslexia or they can expect their children's teachers to do. Like dyslexia itself, this is a complicated area and the information found here cannot cover it all. Therefore, I provide examples of teaching resources (Appendix II). However, remedial work is not the only thing that children with dyslexia need. They also need teachers to adapt and modify what takes place in the classroom in order to bypass the effects of their reading, writing, and related problems. To help in this dialogue between parents and schools, I provide a list of sample classroom accommodations and modifications (Appendix III).

Practical information is not limited to academic issues, however. I believe parents need to know about the other problems that can accompany dyslexia, especially the emotional difficulties and the often-discussed question of whether students with dyslexia should stay back to repeat a grade. Consequently, I include information about these areas. In addition, parents need to know how to explain this disability to their children. To help them with this, I include a list of books written specifically for children of various ages (Appendix II).

In addition, I thought the book should contain information about current issues. Much has been written about the problem people with dyslexia can have understanding how sounds and letters go together. However, this is not the only cause of dyslexia. Consequently, I include chapters about different types of reading disorders. In addition, testing for dyslexia has changed as we have learned more about it, and our understanding of intelligence has moved beyond what many people think of when they hear the words *IQ* or *IQ test*. As a result, I address these areas as well.

What did I leave out? Perhaps the most important omission is information about how parents can negotiate their way through the special education process. This process varies depending on where one lives and changes periodically as laws are rewritten. Consequently, parents need to obtain such information locally. I also chose not to discuss the controversies surrounding how dyslexia and learning disabilities are legally defined. Such definitions also tend to differ depending on where one lives.

It is important to know that the information in this book is not a substitute for either a diagnosis from a qualified professional or education by a skilled teacher. It is also not intended as a legal reference. I do, however, hope that you find it useful.

Finally, although I discuss a few students in this book, names have been changed, information has been altered, and no one should assume to know their identities.

Chapter 1

INTRODUCTION

Tina is a Grade 2 student. She was first identified as needing help when she was in preschool because of her trouble pronouncing words. Although she can remember what she hears without too much difficulty, she is extraordinarily capable at remembering what she sees. Tina also expresses her knowledge much better in a hands-on manner than she does verbally. She knows a lot of information about the world, her math skills are on grade level, and her listening comprehension is fine. However, Tina is able to read only a few words and is completely unable to sound out new ones correctly. She struggled during kindergarten and Grade 1 to learn the names and sounds of letters, and she still is not very sure of them. Despite extra reading instruction and help from a speech/language pathologist, Tina still cannot rhyme adequately, blend sounds together to make words, or break down words into their individual sounds. When she has to name pictures, it can take her up to ten seconds to find some of the words she wants in her long-term memory. Tina has a type of dyslexia.

Dyslexia is a type of *learning disability* (or learning difference) that affects how well someone can read and spell. Researchers have been trying to find out what causes it for a long time and are still working on discovering answers. However, we know much more than we used to.

If someone has dyslexia, it does not mean that she or he cannot read. Everyone with dyslexia can read at least a little. Most people with dyslexia have some words that they can recognize right away. These words are what educators call *sight words* or *sight vocabulary*. Also, many people with dyslexia are able to read words in stories better than they can read them in lists. This is because they have learned to use context to help them figure out words that they do not know or are unsure about. However, good readers do not have to rely on context. They can recognize words no matter where they see them.

Having dyslexia can mean a person has other problems besides difficulty with reading and spelling words correctly. The underlying brain differences that cause dyslexia can also cause problems with reading comprehension, listening, speaking, writing, math, storing information in memory, getting information out of memory, and doing things quickly. In addition, dyslexia can occur with other problems, such as depression, anxiety, *dysgraphia* (a handwriting problem), and various types of attention-deficit/hyperactivity disorder (ADHD).

People with dyslexia do not see words and letters backward. The confusion of similar looking words, letters, and numbers is common in many children as they learn about the symbols we use for writing and math, and they are developmentally normal when children are learning to read. For example, many children struggle with remembering the differences between *b* and *d*, and children with reading problems are no different. For many children with dyslexia, this is a developmental problem connected to their reading level. Many children with dyslexia tend to make letter and word confusions at the same rate as other children with the same reading ability. For example, a ten-year-old child with dyslexia who is reading at a Grade 2 level will probably have the same amount of trouble with *b* and *d* as the average second grade student. However, some types of dyslexia cause children to have this kind of problem for a much longer time. In some cases, they have trouble remembering which letter is which, but if shown a *b* and *d*, for example, they can tell that the letters do not look alike and can copy them correctly. In other cases, their brains send signals to the wrong bit of information. For example, even though they see the word *was* correctly, their brain sometimes sends a signal to the place where the word *saw* is stored.

Information about the occurrence of dyslexia in boys and girls is mixed. Some studies show that reading problems are much more common in boys, while others show little difference based on sex. More boys might be identified with dyslexia because they have a greater tendency than girls to misbehave when they are having trouble, and misbehaving children are more likely to be referred for help.

People with dyslexia are not stupid. In fact, one of the diagnostic requirements is that they have intelligence in the broad average range. All people have things they are good at and other things that they struggle with. People with dyslexia simply struggle with reading and spelling. However, these difficulties create more problems than trouble with other activities such as singing, math, sports, or mechanical skills because reading and spelling are so important in our culture. People who cannot sing well can go through life without anyone ever finding out, but people who struggle with reading or spelling are going to have trouble every day and will find it hard to hide these problems. This can cause low self-esteem and embarrassment. These, in turn, can cause emotional or behavioral problems.

As far as we know, dyslexia cannot be cured, but people with dyslexia can go to college and can be successful. Back in the 1960s, Margaret Rawson (a teacher at a private school in the US) found that even children with severe reading disabilities grew up to be medical doctors, lawyers, educators, entertainers, business owners, scientists, and so on. There is no limit to what people with dyslexia can achieve, but hard work is required. Fortunately, many countries have laws that provide some protections and supports for children and adults with disabilities, including dyslexia.

Chapter 2

CAUSES OF DYSLEXIA

There are two broad categories of dyslexia: acquired and developmental. *Acquired dyslexia* occurs when someone who is a good reader and speller loses at least some of that ability due to a brain injury. For example, a person might have a stroke or be in a car accident. Although this book is not about acquired dyslexia, there are many similarities in the behaviors found in people with acquired and people with developmental dyslexia.

Developmental dyslexia occurs when children have trouble with reading and spelling from the outset. Most children with dyslexia have the developmental type. It seems to be genetic; that is, it tends to run in families, although events such as lead poisoning, head injury, and premature birth can also cause reading problems. However, dyslexia is not 100 percent inherited. In other words, if one parent has it, this does not mean that her or his children will definitely have dyslexia. Also, it can skip around in families. So both parents might be good readers, but one of their children could have dyslexia. Finally, as with many genetic problems, there are combinations of factors that produce dyslexia, some of them inherited and some of them not. This is why one identical twin can have dyslexia while the other does not. It is also one reason why some people are better able to compensate for their reading and spelling problems than others.

Autopsies have shown that developmental dyslexia happens when brain cells get wired in unusual ways. This causes the brains of people with dyslexia to react differently than other people's when they see or hear words. These wiring differences occur before the sixth month of pregnancy. Therefore, children at risk of having dyslexa are born with brains set up to respond differently to words than the brains of children who will most likely become good readers. In some children with a genetic risk of dyslexia, these brain differences may show up in how they respond to speech sounds within the first few months after birth. So, if your child has developmental dyslexia, it probably means that her or his brain is wired a little differently from other people's. There might be too many or too few neurons (brain cells) in one part of the brain, neurons might be connected in an unusual way, or there might be neurons in a part of the brain where they do not belong. However, just as no two people look exactly alike, no two persons' brains are exactly the same either. This is why people have different combinations of strengths and weaknesses. It is also why other people with dyslexia will not be exactly the same as your child. In fact, some reading problems may emerge gradually and not be fully noticed until a child is older, while others will be evident as soon as the child starts trying to learn how to read. Human brains have up to 100 billion neurons, so there is plenty of room for variation.

Researchers have used various types of scanning and imaging machines to look at the brains of people with dyslexia while they listen and read in order to find out what parts of their brains get used. They have found that some parts of the brains of people with dyslexia over-react while other parts under-react compared to the brains of average readers. This shows that the people with dyslexia are *processing* information differently. In other words, their brains try to make sense out of words in a way that makes it harder for them to read and spell. Because there are different foundation skills (also called processing skills) that are important for good reading and spelling, there are different types of dyslexia. Currently, there appear to be five types. These are discussed in the following chapters.

Chapter 3

PHONOLOGICAL DYSLEXIA

A nine-year-old girl was writing a story about a frog, duck, and girl having some adventures. This sentence was part of her story "pesel be klait forg and baky." It says "please be quiet frog and duck." In addition, she pronounces "piano" as "pnano" and "guitar" and "kudar."

Some people with dyslexia have trouble using and making sense out of the sounds that make up words. These sounds are called *phonemes*. People whose reading difficulty is caused by trouble understanding all the different phonemes in words have a weakness in *phonological processing* and are sometimes said to have *phonological dyslexia* or *dysphonetic dyslexia*.

Phonology is the sound structure of a language. Phonological processing refers to how well a person's brain can make sense out of the sounds of language. A weakness in phonological processing can lead to problems with speaking, reading, spelling, and remembering. One important part of phonological processing is *phonemic awareness*. This is the understanding that words are made up of individual sounds. People with good phonemic awareness can hear rhyming words, create rhymes, blend sounds together to make words, and tell how many and what sounds are in words. People with phonological dyslexia struggle with at least some of these skills.

People with phonological dyslexia cannot sound out words very well, so they have trouble reading new words. (The ability to sound out words is what educators call *word attack* or *decoding* and requires an understanding of *phonics*.) Even simple words can cause them trouble. This can make them slow readers.

Some people with phonological dyslexia also mispronounce words when they talk. They might have trouble saying phonemes correctly, drop some sounds from words, or say sounds in the wrong order. For example, they might say *twain* for *train*, *bout* for *about*, *etephone* for *telephone*, *hostipal* for *hospital*, *aminals* for *animals*, or *pasghetti* for *spaghetti*. Of course, most young children make these types of mistakes when they are learning to talk. But some children with phonological processing problems make a greater number of mistakes and the errors can persist after their peers have learned how to say phonemes and words correctly. The nine-year-old girl at the beginning of this chapter has trouble saying some words correctly due to a phonological processing problem.

When people with phonological dyslexia try to spell words, they often add extra sounds, leave out sounds, get sounds in the wrong order, or write down the wrong sounds. For example, they might spell *black* as *back*, *Adam* as *Anad*, *singing* as *sning*, *hospital* as *hosple*, *table* as *talb*, or *bicycle* as *bikl*. Again, such errors are common when children are learning to read and spell. It takes a skilled teacher or evaluator to know if your child's mistakes are signs of a problem. It is hard to read the writing of the nine-year-old girl at the beginning of the chapter because of her trouble getting all the sounds in words correct when she spells.

People with phonological dyslexia can also have trouble remembering exactly what people say. They can remember the general idea or gist okay, but not the specific details. This means that their *verbal memory* can be weak. Some also have trouble correctly interpreting or "hearing" what people say. For example, if you say "Bring out the trash," they might hear "Brian has a rash."

It is important to understand that phonological dyslexia is not caused by poor hearing and cannot be cured with either a hearing aid or tubes. The problem is not in the child's ear, but in how the brain of the child with dyslexia tries to make sense out of the sounds in words. For example, someone with phonological dyslexia might not be able to understand that the word *dog* has three phonemes because they only "hear" the word as a single sound. Think of it this way: if you listen to someone play a chord on the piano (a chord is a combination of three or more notes played at the same time), can you hear and identify all the individual notes, or do you hear just a single sound? For example, if someone played the C-major chord, would you be able to identify that there are three notes and that they are C, E, and G? Unless you are a skilled musician, you probably hear the chord as only a single sound.

People with phonological dyslexia react in a similar way to the sounds in words. They might not be able to figure out that blends like /fl/ or /str/ have more than one phoneme to them, or they might not be able to break down a word like /stop/ into all of its sounds. (The conventional way of showing that someone is referring to speech sounds and not written letters is to use slash marks. So /fl/ refers to the sounds made by these phonemes and not to the written letters.) Their brains do not interpret the sounds in words in sufficient detail. This makes it hard for them to sound out or decode words. This in turn causes trouble with reading and spelling. It can also make it hard for them to get the sounds in long words, like *aluminum*, in the correct order when they speak or write. In addition, it can cause problems with learning the connections between letters and sounds.

What might phonological dyslexia look like in a child? As an example, I will use an eight-year-old girl whom I will call Rachel. Rachel is a quiet and reserved child, but becomes outgoing after she gets to know you. She has a very good sense of humor and laughs easily once she is relaxed. There are no problems with her oral language. That is, she has no trouble either understanding what people say or making herself understood. She also does not have any trouble saying words correctly. She has no problems paying attention and is not hyperactive. She knows an average amount of general information about the world and does not struggle with math.

Rachel can remember both what she sees and what she hears. She has no trouble working quickly and accurately on most things, but she does not always work as carefully as she could. Rachel has some trouble with abstract thinking and problem solving, so her approach to solving problems is to just keep trying until she gets the answer. Her overall IQ score is at the low end of average.

Although Rachel can read almost as many sight words as her peers, she has trouble sounding out new words, and it takes her too long to decode words she should know. Rachel's reading speed is below average because she struggles with letter–sound relationships. She reads words better when they appear in a story than she does when she sees them alone.

Rachel wrote the following story: "The brthta grl is too yr ud to day my drt is too my drt is srt I will giv hra a frow." She read this as: "The birthday girl is two years old today. My daughter is too. My daughter is smart. I will give her a flower." Her writing shows that Rachel has trouble consistently using the sounds of language in an understandable way.

Rachel has trouble recognizing spoken rhyming words. She also cannot adequately identify how many sounds or syllables are in words she hears. These are phonological processing problems and the cause of her reading and spelling difficulties.

Chapter 4

ORTHOGRAPHIC DYSLEXIA

While writing a story, a ten-year-old boy wrote the following words: onere (owner), hav (have), cretchirs (creatures), grabed (grabbed), bildings (buildings), colect (collect), and arkialijest (archeologist).

Some people with dyslexia are able to work with the sounds of language but have trouble remembering what letters or words look like. They do not see letters and words backward, but they might have trouble remembering how to tell the difference between the letters *b, d*, and *p*. They might also confuse words that look alike, such as *was* and *saw, who* and *how, thought* and *through*, and *young* and *youth*. People who have trouble remembering what words and letters look like have trouble with *orthographic processing* and are sometimes said to have *orthographic dyslexia, surface dyslexia, or dyseidetic dyslexia*.

Orthography refers to the spelling and writing systems of a language. In English these are the letters, letter combinations, and irregular words we use for writing. Orthographic processing refers to how well people's brains make sense out of written numerals, letters, and words. While phonological processing deals with the sounds of language, orthographic processing deals with the written symbols of language. It is the visual part of reading and writing. Problems with orthographic processing can lead to trouble with reading, spelling, and math.

Just as there is phonemic awareness, there is also orthographic awareness. This is the understanding that written language is comprised of spelling patterns that are larger than individual letters. English has many of these, such as *ough, ow, ight, th, kn*, and so on.

Some people with orthographic dyslexia have trouble remembering the differences between *homophones*. Homophones are words that sound the same but are spelled differently and have different meanings. For example, *pane* and *pain* are homophones. Reading homophones does not help people know which meaning is relevant because the words are pronounced the same way. The only way to know the meanings of homophones (when there is no context to help you) is to recognize the way the words look. You can think of this as a type of visual memory. People with orthographic dyslexia frequently confuse homophones in their writing.

Orthographic dyslexia can also cause trouble with irregular words. Irregular words (which are sometimes called exception words) are words that cannot be sounded out because they are not spelled exactly the way they are pronounced. Think of the words *said* and *broad*. If we pronounced these words according to the rules, we would read them as /sade/ and /brode/. People with orthographic dyslexia often make these types of mistakes. They understand the sounds of words and they understand the ways letters and sounds go together, but they have trouble when the letters and sounds do not match. Irregular words, just like homophones, require a good visual memory. Some of the most common words in English are irregular words. Examples are *what, who, there, one, does,* and *come*.

Unlike people with phonological dyslexia, people with orthographic dyslexia are often very good at reading new words as long as those words follow the rules about how letters and sounds are supposed to work. They can even sound out long words like *apparatus* or *astronomer*, although they might get the accent in the wrong place or divide the syllables incorrectly.

People with orthographic processing problems often read more slowly and make more errors when there are a lot of words on a page. They might also skip lines when they read. The more words there are and the closer together they are, the more trouble some people with orthographic dyslexia have visually processing them.

The problems that people with orthographic dyslexia have with similar looking letters, such as *b* and *d*, can persist into their teenage years and beyond. They often use capital letters when they write so they do not get confused. For example, they might spell *trouble* as *trouBle*. People with orthographic dyslexia can also confuse numbers that look alike (such as *2* and *5* or *15* and *51*).

When people with orthographic processing problems spell words they usually get all the sounds written down but do not use the correct letters. For example, they might spell *said* as *sed*, *thought* as *thot*, *make* as *mack*, or *each* as *ech*. Other examples are found in the spellings of the ten-year-old boy at the beginning of this chapter. They can hear the sounds but cannot remember how the words look. Because they can hear the sounds in words, they sometimes spell in unusual ways, such as spelling *example* as *egzampl* or *archeologist* as *arkialijest*, as the boy at the beginning of the chapter did. They may also confuse the order of letters in words. For instance, they might be able to remember all the letters in the word *two* but be unable to recall if the *w* or the *o* comes first. Alternatively, they might remember that *-able* is a common way for words to end but be unable to remember if it is spelled *able* or *abel*, since the *e* is silent. Sometimes they spell the same word two or more different ways in the same piece of writing because they cannot remember how it is supposed to look.

It is important to understand that orthographic dyslexia is not caused by poor vision and cannot be cured with eyeglasses. The problem is not with the child's eyes, but in how the brain of the child with dyslexia tries to make sense out of the letters in words.

What might orthographic dyslexia look like in a child? As an example, I will use a 14-year-old boy whom I will call Bruce. Bruce says he likes school, but his favorite activities are the nonacademic times of day such as recess, gym, art, and music. His hearing and eyesight are average and he has not had any serious illnesses. However, he did break his leg recently in a snowboarding accident. Bruce has good oral language skills and does not have any trouble paying attention. He has a positive attitude and accepts his disability as a part of who he is.

Bruce knows a lot of information about the world, can remember what he hears, has a good vocabulary, and is able to solve problems at an average level. He has no trouble making sense out of what he sees (*visual perception*) and his *spatial skills* are good. This means he has no trouble working with spaces, such as avoiding bumping into things, leaving the same amount of room between words when he writes, and getting numbers lined up when he copies math problems. Bruce can remember how things look as long as those things are not letters, words, or numbers. Overall, these abilities give him an IQ at the low end of average.

Bruce's oral reading is slow and labored. For example, he reads Grade 3 material with a speed of only 40 words per minute when the average reading speed for someone his age is at least three times as fast for much harder material. Bruce's knowledge of sight words is below average, but he can sound out long words as long as they follow the rules. For example, he was slow but accurate at decoding the words *interested* and *astronomer*. Even slower, however, is Bruce's skill at recognizing irregular words such as *through* and *prove*. He uses context to help him read. Therefore, Bruce reads more words correctly in stories than he does when they appear alone.

Bruce sometimes writes numbers backward, but usually catches these mistakes and corrects them. He often carries the wrong number when adding, but his overall math skills are average.

Bruce's ability to express ideas in writing is average, but his spelling is poor. When he spells, Bruce confuses homophones such as *their* and *there*, *threw* and *through*, and *brake* and *break*. He spells words the way they sound, not the way they look. He sometimes confuses the order of letters in words or mixes up similar looking letters. Examples of his spelling mistakes are listed below. Bruce's mistakes are easy to read because he gets all the sounds correct.

Bruce's spelling	Correct spelling
villeg	village
spers	spears
prity	pretty
tung	tongue
wer	were
vacashun	vacation
ulike	alike
beacuse	because
whith	with
palincing	balancing

Bruce has no trouble retrieving most types of information from his *long-term memory*, and is able to work with the sounds of language without difficulty. The fact that Bruce can sound out words that follow the rules and has no trouble hearing sounds in words, but confuses words based on how they look, shows that he has a problem with orthographic processing but not with phonological processing. His processing problem is the cause of his reading and spelling difficulties.

Chapter 5

RETRIEVAL PROBLEMS

(ALSO CALLED "RAPID NAMING" DEFICITS)

Some people with dyslexia have trouble easily retrieving information from their long-term memory. For some, this happens only when they are reading or spelling and is limited to symbols like letters, numbers, and printed words. For others, however, the *retrieval problems* are broader and include difficulty finding other information in their memory such as the names of objects or people, math facts, dates, the sounds of letters, and so on. Because they have trouble retrieving words, letters, or sounds, these people with dyslexia are slow readers. This means they are *rate disabled*. They often read all the words correctly, but it takes them a lot longer than average to get through the material. People who cannot read quickly because of retrieval problems know the words and letters; they just cannot find that information in their memory quickly. In addition, they might know a word in one sentence but not recall it when they see it again in the next sentence or on the next page.

People who read slowly often have trouble remembering and comprehending what they read. They spend so much time and exert so much energy reading the words correctly that they do not have enough processing or memory capacity left to make sense out of the text.

At times when some people with retrieval problems talk, they describe things because they cannot think of the exact words. For example, they might know the word *escalator*, but while talking about a visit to the shopping mall they might call it the *moving stairs*. As with reading, people with retrieval problems might be able to recall a word one time but have trouble a few days, or even a few minutes, later. Even simple words, like the names of common objects (*key*, *cow*), can get lost in their memory at times. Everyone has trouble with this once in awhile, and we call it the "tip of the tongue" experience. For example, you

27

might see someone in the grocery store and be aware that you know her or his name, but not remember it until you are driving home several minutes later. People with retrieval problems can experience this kind of difficulty more often. It can be frustrating because they know that they know the words; they just cannot always think of them when they need to.

Instead of describing things, people with retrieval problems might pause when they talk as they try to think of the words they want. Sometimes these pauses can last for a long time, such as 5, 10, 15 or more seconds, as they search their memory for the right words. At other times, they might use nonspecific words like *thing* or *stuff* because they cannot find the correct words in their memory.

Retrieval problems related to reading are usually evaluated with tests that look at *rapid naming*. These tests ask children or adults to look at letters, numbers, colors, or pictures of common objects and name them as fast as they can. The reason for using these tests is to find out how automatic people are at retrieving simple information. If it takes them a long time to find easy, overly-learned information, like letter names, in their memory, it will also take them a long time to find other words.

What might a retrieval problem look like in a child? Here is an example, a nine-year-old boy whom I will call Frank. Frank is a sociable boy who enjoys trying to manipulate situations to his advantage and who tries to take control whenever he can. He can have trouble paying attention. It is very easy to strike up a conversation with Frank, and he has no trouble understanding what people say. Sometimes he is slow to think of what he wants to say, but this does not happen very often.

Frank likes to play with building bricks and enjoys video games. He has excellent visual perception and spatial skills. On a test where he had to copy abstract block designs and put puzzles together, he not only did a good job but also earned bonus points for getting the right answers quickly. When he has to solve visual problems, Frank works in a methodical manner and is able to picture correct solutions in his head before he begins. Because of skills like these, Frank's overall IQ is above average.

Frank completes much of his schoolwork quickly and without difficulty. He has no trouble figuring out how to solve math word problems and knows how to do the computations, but he is slow at recalling math facts. His copying is very slow, even for simple information, and his oral reading is *dysfluent*; that is, he does not read smoothly. Frank's reading is slow, he makes lots of mistakes on easy words, he does not pause in the right places or phrase sentences well, and he tends to ignore punctuation. Frank also does not read with much expression in his voice. However, he can read an average number of sight words and can sound out new words with average skill.

Frank knows a lot of information about the world and is able to use that information to think at higher levels. If you read things to him, he can understand them at a level well above his peers. However, Frank's reading comprehension is not as high as his listening comprehension because of his trouble with reading fluency.

Frank can write well, and his spelling is average. On memory tests, he had no trouble either repeating what he heard or remembering what he saw. However, he struggled when he had to learn the names of children because he had a considerable difficulty remembering what names went with what faces.

Frank has good phonological and orthographic processing. His trouble centers on recalling specific information and recalling it quickly. This is affecting his reading, speaking, copying, paired learning (such as matching the names of children to their faces and the names of countries to their shapes), and makes him slow in math. He is considered rate disabled because of his retrieval problem.

Chapter 6

DEEP DYSLEXIA

A very rare form of developmental dyslexia is called *deep dyslexia*. An important sign of deep dyslexia is when people make frequent *semantic* (that is, meaning) substitutions as they read words in a list. They misread small words (called *function words*), such as reading *are* for *all*, *through* for *after*, or *at* for *in*. They also make errors by saying a word that is somehow associated with the one they are looking at. For example, they might read *merry* as *Christmas* or *ice cream* as *cone*. In addition, they make coordinate errors. These are mistakes where the words share a similar meaning, such as reading *tulip* for *rose*, *jump* for *run*, *comb* for *brush*, or *mother* for *cousin*. The reading mistakes that deep dyslexics make do not share much sight or sound overlap with the words they are looking at. For example, *mother* and *cousin* do not share either many of the same letters or many of the same sounds, but they overlap in meaning.

It is important for diagnosis that these errors show up when children read words in a list and not just when they are reading a story or book. Many young and poor readers substitute words when they read text. They do this because they are trying to predict words based on context. This is not a sign of deep dyslexia, but it is an indication of weak reading skills.

People with deep dyslexia tend to read concrete nouns best and function words worst (concrete nouns are nouns that can be easily pictured like *hammer*, *ocean*, and *car*). They have a hard time decoding words, but can have good speaking vocabularies.

Morag Stuart and David Howard (1995) described a 13-year-old girl with developmental deep dyslexia. They called the girl KJ. Some of KJ's reading mistakes are listed below. These types of mistake also showed up when KJ talked.

Written word	What KJ read
boy	man
came	go
children	friends
hurt	accident
kicked	ball
play	friends
kitten	ball
light	radio

KJ was unable to sound out any three-letter nonwords (like *mab*). When someone said a sound, KJ could pick the letter that went with it, but when shown a letter she had a great deal of trouble coming up with the correct sound. She was better at writing letters when people said their names than she was at naming letters that people pointed to. However, she did poorly on both of these tasks.

Linda Siegel (1985) described six seven-year-old and eight-year-old children with deep dyslexia. Like KJ, they could not sound out nonwords, had average listening vocabularies, and made semantic errors when reading words in a list. Siegel made an important contrast between the kinds of mistakes poor or young readers make and the kinds of mistakes people with deep dyslexia make. A beginning reader might look at *chicken* and read it as *children* because the words look a lot alike. On the other hand, someone with deep dyslexia might look at the word *chicken* and read it as *eagle* because of a coordinate error.

As I stated at the beginning of this chapter, this is a very rare type of dyslexia. Counting my years spent teaching and doing evaluations, I have spent approximately 30 years working with reading disabled students but I have not yet encountered anyone with deep dyslexia.

Chapter 7

MIXED AND OTHER DYSLEXIAS

Many (and perhaps most) people with dyslexia have trouble reading and writing because of multiple processing problems. They have *mixed dyslexia* and are probably the ones who will have the hardest time learning to read and spell. One person might have trouble with both phonological and orthographic processing. Someone else might have trouble with orthographic processing and rapid naming. A third person might have trouble with all three types of processing. In addition, there is some overlap in characteristics among the different types. For example, people with phonological dyslexia and those who are rate disabled can both have trouble with verbal memory, and people with all types of dyslexia can be slow readers or know a word on one page of text but not on the next because they do not have context-free recognition for it.

Researchers are still discovering things about dyslexia. There may be more types than the ones mentioned in this book. For example, some recent research indicates that people with dyslexia might have trouble processing things that happen quickly. Some might not "hear" rapid phonemes such as /b/ or /p/. These sounds tend to explode; that is, they happen very fast and cannot be drawn out the way other sounds can, like /m/ and /l/. Other people with dyslexia might have trouble seeing things correctly when they move. For example, they might see words all right when they stare at them, but when they move their eyes to scan across a page the words and letters might get confused. We do not know much about these types of processing problems. They might be related to phonological and orthographic processing, they might represent other types of processing and other types of dyslexia, or they might not even really exist. Researchers are still trying to figure it out.

What might mixed dyslexia look like in a child? One example is a 13-year-old middle-school girl whom I will call Louise. Louise is an outgoing student who routinely gets average or better grades. She has great social skills with both peers and adults and has excellent oral language skills. She is known as a good problem solver, likes sports, but never reads unless she has to. She does not have any problems paying attention and always gives careful thought to things before making decisions. No one expressed concerns about her academic skills before she reached middle school and she has never been a behavior problem.

Louise scored average to above average on an IQ test. She possesses a great deal of knowledge and knows how to use it. If you give her problems of a kind she has not seen before, she is able to solve them better than most of her peers. Louise also has good visual perception, but her ability to remember what she hears is at the low end of average. Because most of her other cognitive skills are higher, this makes verbal memory a personal weakness for her. She is also low average in working with the sounds in words. Therefore, Louise has a mild phonological processing problem. This is one reason why her word reading skills are slightly below average.

Louise has a lot of trouble remembering what words look like and often confuses homophones. Some of her spelling mistakes are *wethe* for *whether*, *foloing* for *following*, *wurst* for *worst*, and *anething* for *anything*. As you can see, she does not have much trouble getting the sounds correct when she spells, but she uses the wrong letters. Her spelling is at a Grade 3 level, but the ideas she writes, the language she uses, and the grammar of her written work are all on grade level. Louise shows signs of having a significant orthographic processing problem.

Louise is also a slow reader. She reads only about 50 words per minute at the Grade 4 level when someone her age should be able to read harder material over three times as fast. Also, Louise makes a lot of mistakes as she reads. Her mistakes include omitting endings from verbs (for example, leaving the letter *s* off *stops*), leaving out small words like *the* and *a*, and adding words that make sense based on context but that are not in the book. However, she has no trouble understanding what she reads.

Although Louise can do simple visual tasks with average speed, such as finding matching shapes, she cannot look at and name letters or single-digit numbers quickly. She is also very slow recalling math facts and has been unable to memorize many of them. This affects her arithmetic more than her math problem solving. In addition to Louise's phonological and orthographic difficulties, she has trouble retrieving information from her long-term memory.

Louise's mild problem with phonological processing coupled with her significant trouble with both orthographic processing and naming speed show that she has mixed dyslexia. She has been somewhat able to compensate for it on her own, but her reading speed and spelling remain very poor. She has a mild to moderate reading disorder along with a severe spelling disability.

Another example of someone with mixed dyslexia is a 12-year-old whom I will call Richard. Richard has been in *special education* since kindergarten. He does not like school and has some emotional problems both because of his learning difficulties and because of traumas he experienced when younger. His emotions can change quickly and he tends to give up easily. On the other hand, Richard can be encouraged to try and works well with people who are able to establish a good relationship with him. His oral language skills are good and he does not have any problems paying attention. He also is not impulsive. He enjoys computer games, television, movies, and individual sports (such as skating).

Richard has a good knowledge base and an IQ at the upper end of average. His listening comprehension is average, but his reading comprehension is poor because he struggles to read. Math, social studies, and science are his best academic areas and he is currently doing average work in all three. When he tries to read words in a list, Richard makes both phonological and orthographic errors. That is, he adds sounds, leaves out sounds, recalls incorrect sounds for some letters, gets sounds in the wrong order, and does not recognize some common spelling patterns. He makes similar mistakes when he reads text and also leaves out words and adds words that are not on the page. Richard reads slowly and makes a lot of mistakes, which he does not often correct. His reading level is Grade 2, but even at that level he reads poorly.

Richard's writing is hard to read because so many of the words are indecipherable. Like his reading, Richard's spelling shows signs of both phonological and orthographic difficulties. He leaves out sounds, leaves out syllables, tries to spell words the way they sound, reverses *b* and *d*, confuses sounds, confuses homophones, spells words more than one way, and has trouble remembering how words look. Some of his spelling errors are listed below along with an example of his writing.

Richard's spelling	Correct spelling
fist	first
hardy	hardly
sdly	suddenly
sintis	scientist
hptol	hospital
trid	tried
lafe	laugh
bue	dude
tocod	tackled
averwon	everyone
Apirl	April
here	hear

Mark hite somethin hird. He on barits he haller "Ataft" Mark say "the hammis live hear befor we got hear." Ciny say "maybe or the Ainte trid ot sode "su be fow we did."

Richard's reading and spelling errors along with his test scores show significant problems with phonological processing, orthographic processing, and rapid naming/retrieval. Therefore, he has mixed dyslexia. His is a severe case.

Chapter 8

OTHER INFORMATION ABOUT DYSLEXIA AND PEOPLE WITH DYSLEXIA

The mixed dyslexia cases of Louise and Richard show that just as there are different levels of ability (for example, novice, intermediate, expert), there are different levels of dyslexia. Some people have mild cases. They might not be noticed at school until the upper grades and some might never get diagnosed. Some have moderate cases and some, like Richard, have severe dyslexia. Some might have a mild or moderate problem with reading but a severe problem with spelling, as Louise has. There are also people who are good readers but poor spellers. However, they are typically not considered as having dyslexia.

Sometimes people with dyslexia also have trouble with other things, such as writing neatly, being organized, and expressing their ideas in writing beyond just trouble with spelling. Some of these problems might be caused by dysgraphia. Dysgraphia is not just messy handwriting. It is a problem with the physical act of writing and like dyslexia comes in different degrees of difficulty. Some children with dysgraphia might not be able to hold a pencil correctly while others might be able to hold a pencil but be unable to draw a line. Some people with dysgraphia can write letters only as a series of disconnected movements. Others learn how to write letters but their handwriting is only legible if they write very slowly.

The difference between writing problems due to dyslexia and writing problems caused by dysgraphia is important to recognize. Doris Johnson and Helmer Myklebust back in 1967 offered an excellent explanation. Children with dysgraphia know what they want to write, but cannot develop the motor plan to create it, even if the letters, words, or shapes are right in front of them.

Therefore, they are unable to copy. On the other hand, children with dyslexia are physically able to copy, but might have trouble writing due to less severe fine motor problems, difficulty with reading and spelling, or memory deficits.

People with dyslexia can also have trouble with math. For instance, they might misread numerals, have trouble remembering math facts, or copy numerals incorrectly. Other areas that might cause problems for people with dyslexia are memory, organization, following complex verbal directions, remembering left and right, and learning a foreign language. Nevertheless, although dyslexia can cause various difficulties for people who have it, there are things they can do well.

Everyone is good at some things and not very good at others. People with dyslexia are no different and are probably found in almost every profession. According to websites such as www.dyslexia.com/qafame.htm, there have been some famous people who either had dyslexia or had symptoms of dyslexia, such as Leonardo da Vinci, Nelson Rockefeller, Thomas Edison, Hans Christian Andersen, Sir Winston Churchill, and Agatha Christie. These people were artists, politicians, inventors, and authors. One (Winston Churchill) was Prime Minister of Great Britain and another (Nelson Rockefeller) was a US Vice President.

Margaret Rawson (1995) followed a group of people with dyslexia for 55 years, from their elementary education at a small, private US school in the 1930s and 1940s to their adult lives in the 1990s. The dyslexic men in her study were just as successful as their nondisabled classmates. There were as many skilled laborers and professionals among the people with dyslexia as there were among the men without reading and writing disabilities. In addition, equal numbers of men with and without dyslexia went to college and obtained Master's and Doctor's degrees. The men with dyslexia did attend college for a slightly longer time than their classmates. They might have needed extra time to earn their degrees, or perhaps they were motivated to study longer. On the other hand, in 2000 the US government found that about 30 percent of disabled students (some of whom undoubtedly had dyslexia) dropped out of school.

As with any disability, dyslexia can lead to social, emotional, and behavioral difficulties. These include trouble with peers, anxiety, depression, and insecurity. Denial, anger, guilt, shame, and fear can be common emotional responses before people reach a level of acceptance about the disability. Social, emotional, and behavioral difficulties can show up in the person with dyslexia and in family members. For instance, the person with dyslexia might be angry or depressed about her or his reading problems. She or he might also be resentful of how well brothers and sisters do and the praise they receive. Alternatively, siblings can become jealous about the extra attention the child with dyslexia receives. They can experience negative thoughts about having a disabled sibling, and can be angry about what they might see as double standards. For example, the child with dyslexia might be given extra support at home or school, have modified assignments that appear to be less work, or receive more praise from parents for good grades than their brother or sister gets.

Surprisingly, despite their children's struggles, many parents are not ready for the diagnosis when it arrives. When parents receive the news that their child has dyslexia, they might be angry, mourn the loss of a "perfect" child, or deny that there is a problem. Conflicts between spouses and in-laws can increase after the diagnosis depending on how the news is received and interpreted, or if the diagnosis is even accepted.

On the other hand, finally knowing what is wrong and why a child or sibling is struggling can bring a feeling of relief for everyone. It can end family conflicts, guilt, and blaming; and it can allow some families to begin healing and moving on. It can also raise awareness about and acceptance for disabilities and differences, as well as encourage siblings to be supportive of each other.

All people are different. It has been said that we all live in a world with only one inhabitant because no one, not even a person's siblings, has had exactly the same experiences as that person has. We all have our own personality and unique experiences in life, and we all react in different ways to what happens to us. Similarly, no two people will have the same emotional reaction to having dyslexia. However, the experiences of adults who grew up struggling to read reveal some of what it is like for people with reading problems. Not surprisingly, these experiences have been both positive and negative. Much of the following information is based on Michael A. McNulty's (2003) article, "Dyslexia and the life course."

Adults with dyslexia report that they knew they were different from other children. Some knew this before they started school, perhaps because they had trouble saying words correctly. Others knew it as early as kindergarten or Grade 1 when they were unable to learn letters and sounds as well as their classmates. Many adults say that their trouble in school made them feel ashamed and stupid. Some thought they were lazy and incapable of trying hard enough to learn. Many say that their school problems gave them low self-esteem.

Some adults say that they made it through elementary school without too much trouble, but when they reached middle school they began to doubt their intelligence. Some felt alone in the struggle to learn how to read because their friends and siblings were not having trouble. Some say they would sometimes get home from school and cry in frustration at not understanding what the teacher was saying about reading and spelling. Being forced to read aloud in class could be humiliating and make them feel ashamed. Being referred and tested because of their school problems was traumatic for some since it reinforced the feeling that there was something wrong with them or that they were stupid. However, others found it a relief to know that adults were concerned and wanted to find out how to help.

Parents and teachers who did not understand their problems made the children with dyslexia feel worse about themselves. On the other hand, this gave some of them the motivation to try harder even though the cost of doing well at school was extra hours of studying that took time away from friends and nonacademic activities. Some were embarrassed by having to get extra help in school, but others felt relief at knowing that they were not stupid, that they were not alone, and that their reading problems were not their fault. Teachers and other adults who accepted the children for who they were provided many positive experiences for them.

Some adults with dyslexia report that they denied having any kind of trouble and rebelled in middle or high school, finding relief from their academic problems in parties, risk taking, truancy, and other inappropriate behaviors. However, more seem to have looked early on for ways to succeed. They found success in areas such as sports, art, dance, theater, mechanical skills, or a social life. These accomplishments increased their self-esteem, and they later realized they were the first steps to finding a way to build a successful career. Some people with dyslexia settled for lower level classes in high school, but others took college preparatory courses and had support and help from parents or tutors.

Some adults say that having test results and dyslexia explained to them in positive ways was very important to them as children. Others say that not having adults explain things meant they were left to imagine the worst. Counseling to deal with the emotional impact of having a disability was necessary for some. Understanding parents and teachers helped a lot, as did a school environment that acknowledged differences and allowed children to find ways to succeed.

Music, band, art, home economics, computer classes, "shop," physical education, and other nonacademic classes are important for students with dyslexia because they can provide them with ways to succeed. Allowing students different ways to show their learning, such as through projects or oral tests instead of written work, can also help children and teens to maintain good self-esteem, although others are embarrassed at not being treated the same as their classmates. No one approach will work for everyone. Schools and parents have to work together to meet the unique needs of each child.

Their life experiences have left some adults with dyslexia overly sensitive to criticism while others have accepted themselves for who they are. Some adults with dyslexia feel they gave up too easily and settled for lesser jobs than they are capable of. Some still question their intelligence. Some harbor resentments against peers who made fun of them or teachers who did not understand them. Other adults with dyslexia say that they went to college and made an all-out effort to do well. They have either found success in spite of their disability or discovered careers where their disability does not get in the way. Some have found ways to make the most of their talents and now look at their dyslexia as a difference instead of a disability. They believe this difference gives them unique ways of thinking about things. Some even consider dyslexia to be a gift. However, reading, spelling, penmanship, and the other difficulties that go along with dyslexia are still problems for them, and they accept the fact that their dyslexia cannot be cured.

Overall, the life experiences of people with dyslexia match the life experiences of almost everyone else. Most adults have had both good and bad teachers, were teased or bullied about something, felt that siblings were treated better than they were in some way, doubted their ability in some area, and needed to work extra hard to learn some skills. Most people also need to overcome or compensate for personal weaknesses, find careers that match their skills, learn to accept themselves for who they are, and learn to let go of childhood insults and injuries.

Despite these broad similarities, however, the struggle that children with dyslexia have with reading and spelling can be traumatic (to use the word that some dyslexic adults use). Every day for 12 or more years they have to spend six to seven hours at school coming face to face with things they cannot do very well – and they need to do this in front of their peers. This would be hard for anyone to deal with, even adults, and there is no question that any disability creates hardships for the person who has it. However, as I noted in Chapter 1, problems with reading and spelling are particularly troublesome because these skills are so important in our culture.

Chapter 9

DIAGNOSIS AND EVALUATION

As you have decided to read this book, someone you know has probably already been evaluated and found to have dyslexia. Regardless, it is important for you to know that there is no such thing as a dyslexia test. Dyslexia can only be diagnosed by a skilled person or team of people who have the right types of tests and who are knowledgeable about learning and disabilities.

Because dyslexia has to do with trouble in reading and spelling, it cannot be diagnosed until after someone has had the chance to become a good reader and speller. Therefore, although a child in preschool, kindergarten, Grade 1, or even Grade 2 might have trouble with phonemes or struggle to learn letters, that does not necessarily mean that she or he has dyslexia. Some children just take longer to acquire one or more skills. Such children have *developmental delays* and usually outgrow them with some help.

A developmental delay happens when a child acquires one or more skills at a slower pace than is typical. This might be because part of the child's brain is developing at a slower rate than average or because the child has not had as much practice with some skills as other children. Some children with developmental delays are at risk of having reading and spelling problems, but they do not have dyslexia. Children with dyslexia will continue to have trouble and will not just grow out of it. They can learn to read and spell better, but it takes a great deal of extra work. They usually need to be taught differently and will probably always have some type of reading and spelling trouble. Even adults who have learned to compensate for their dyslexia still tend to read slowly and struggle with spelling.

What kinds of tests might be included in an evaluation to find out if a child has dyslexia? There are many and the choice of tests is up to the qualified person doing the evaluation. Although there are some types of tests that are likely to be used, do not be fooled by people who say that a particular test must be used.

One kind of test that is likely to show up in an evaluation is an IQ or intelligence test. There is a lot of misunderstanding about IQs and intelligence. Therefore, I will discuss this type of test more than any other.

There are many different ways to be intelligent and no test looks at all of them. In fact, not everyone agrees on what intelligence is or how it should be measured. One current theory states that there are seven different types of intelligence and that these types are not related to each other. These types of intelligence are reasoning and math, mastery of language, manipulating and creating mental images, musical ability, coordinated body movements, understanding oneself, and understanding and getting along with others. IQ tests do not measure most of these skills.

Other people think that creativity, wisdom, and common sense (or "street smarts") are important aspects of intelligence. IQ tests do not usually look at these skills either.

Much has been written lately about emotional intelligence. This includes knowing and managing your emotions, motivating yourself, hanging on when things get tough, controlling your impulses, waiting to get what you want, maintaining the ability to think in the face of distress, recognizing emotions in others, feeling for others, and handling relationships. IQ tests do not measure these skills.

Some IQ tests are based on the theory that there are eight to ten types of intelligence that are all related to each other. These types of intelligence are solving unique problems, learning facts about the world and using that information to solve problems, memory and learning, visual perception (that is, making sense out of what you see), auditory perception (that is, making sense out of sounds), retrieving information from memory, working quickly, thinking quickly, reading and writing, and math. No IQ test measures all of these, but some measure many of these skills. But think about yourself for a minute. Are you equally skilled at all of these? Probably not. Therefore, it is not surprising that most children do not perform the same in all areas.

In addition, each of the above areas can be tested in many different ways. For example, according to experts, auditory perception could be tested in any of the following ways: identifying speech sounds, hearing speech in distracting environments, understanding distorted speech, determining which direction a sound came from, hearing or identifying the differences in musical pitches or tones, or maintaining a musical beat. These are only some of the ways to test this type of intelligence. Now think about people with phonological processing problems. They might do well on the auditory processing part of an IQ test that asks them to work with musical tones but fail if they have to work with speech sounds. On the other hand, people who are tone deaf but do not have dyslexia might succeed if the test involves speech sounds but do poorly if musical tones are involved. Therefore, the way an ability is tested can affect how well someone does on an IQ test.

Every IQ test measures intelligence in different ways. Every IQ test looks at different combinations of skills, and every IQ test fails to measure some types of intelligent behavior. So how can someone's intelligence be summed up in a single number, an IQ test score? It cannot.

You should also remember that how well people do on any type of test, including an IQ test, can be affected by a lot of different things. Some of these are their natural abilities, the environment in which they were raised, the environment in which the test is given, and their educational background (both formal and informal). Other influences include motivation, interest, health, developmental processes, culture, and familiarity with the language and expectations of the test. Still more things that can affect someone's test score are temperament, comfort level with guessing and uncertainty, attention span, motor skills, and the ability to work both under close scrutiny and without the type of supportive feedback typically given in school settings. Even more influential conditions are emotional factors, the perceived importance of the test, examiner/test-taker interactions, and interfering disabilities.

How can a disability interfere with someone's performance on an IQ test? There are many ways. The most obvious ways are easily observed. For example, children with poor motor skills might have trouble if they have to use a pencil, manipulate blocks, do puzzles, and so on. In addition, children with reading disorders might not do well if the IQ test requires them to read. However, there is a more pervasive but often overlooked effect of reading disabilities on IQ test performance. This effect is called the Matthew effect. A researcher named Keith Stanovich (1986) coined this term after the Christian biblical story in the book of Matthew about the rich getting richer and the poor getting poorer. Research shows that children with reading problems (such as dyslexia) spend less time reading and read lower level materials than their peers. Therefore, they are exposed to fewer words, learn less vocabulary, and encounter a smaller number of new ideas. This can have a snowballing effect, which, over time, causes these children to learn less and less new information. As a result, their scores on some parts of IQ tests tend to decline. These children are not getting dumber. Their disabilities are simply interfering with their achievement, and that, in turn, affects how well they do on some of the tasks commonly found on intelligence tests. Unfortunately, this decrease in learning has been found to extend into adulthood.

It is also important to know that people's IQ scores do not determine their fate. IQ test scores account for only about 25 percent of how well people do in school and even less of their success in adult life. In addition, that 25 percent can drop to as low as 10 percent when performance in isolated academic skills is examined. But intelligence tests (or cognitive tests as I prefer to call them) can tell us important information about people's strengths and weaknesses. Therefore, they can be an informative part of an evaluation. They just need to be used and interpreted properly.

In addition to one or more cognitive tests, a dyslexia evaluation should include some type of processing tests. The separation of skills into cognitive and processing areas is sort of random since most skills probably fit into both categories. All higher level cognitive tasks involve some types of processing. However, the basic processing skills likely to be looked at in a dyslexia evaluation are the ones discussed in this book: phonological processing, orthographic processing, and rapid naming.

Phonological processing might be looked at by having the child rhyme, identify the number of words in spoken sentences, or mentally manipulate the sounds in words. Orthographic processing might be tested by having the child look at and remember letters or words, identify homophones, or read and spell both regular and irregular words. Rapid naming might require that the child look at and name letters, numbers, or pictured objects as fast as possible. Other processing areas that might be tested include how easily a child can get information out of her or his memory without having something to look at (this is called retrieval fluency) and how quickly she or he can work in general (a type of processing speed).

There are different levels of phonological and orthographic processing and different types of rapid naming tasks. Not all people with processing problems do poorly on all of them. For example, someone with phonological dyslexia might do well on a sound blending task in which she or he listens to individual sounds and has to identify the whole word (for example, identifying the sound sequence /s/-/t/-/o/-/p/ as /stop/), but be unable to manipulate sounds in words (for example, saying/blend/without the /l/). Also, someone with a retrieval problem might have no difficulty naming colors rapidly but have significant trouble naming letters. Knowledgeable evaluators know about these differences and do their best to make sure processing difficulties are not overlooked.

No dyslexia evaluation can take place without an examination of reading and writing. This might include spelling from dictation, creative writing, reading a list of real words, sounding out a list of nonsense words, reading stories aloud, and some kind of reading comprehension test. A listening comprehension test might also be involved as might an examination of math skills. In addition, some evaluators explore how well students understand the structure of stories, which is called *story grammar*. To do this, they might ask them to listen to and retell stories, create oral stories from wordless books, or write stories from prompts.

Evaluators sometimes like to look at visual and verbal memory. Some examine how well the child can speak and express ideas orally. Some might also look at what are called *executive functions*. These are skills that help us regulate our behaviors and emotions, allow us to plan, and let us use our intelligence. Some evaluators screen for behavioral, emotional, and developmental problems. This can be particularly important because many students with dyslexia also have other difficulties that need to be addressed. Finally, family and medical history might also be part of the evaluation.

Family and historical information can offer an important understanding of the context in which the student's problems developed. As a result, it can offer insights into things such as the likelihood of other problems (emotional, behavioral, learning) being present and offer information about the likely course and treatment for the student's problems. For example, there is evidence that the ability to compensate for dyslexia runs in families and the treatments that worked for other family members might offer insight into good approaches to use with the student being evaluated. In addition, family information can help teachers work with parents better. For example, it might be discovered that a parent also has a learning problem (perhaps not yet diagnosed) that causes him or her to have negative attitudes toward school and not (or not be able to) follow up with reading and spelling activities at home. By learning about this, the student's teachers will have a better understanding of how to work with the parent.

Sometimes it takes only one person to do an evaluation. This person might be a type of psychologist or educational diagnostician. Other times a team of people is involved, such as an educational psychologist, clinical psychologist, special educator, speech/language pathologist, and occupational therapist.

The point of an evaluation is to discover or confirm your child's strengths and weaknesses. Knowing this information is more important than having your child labeled with dyslexia. That diagnosis alone does not identify what needs to be done to help her or him. Some professionals are uncomfortable using the word dyslexia or hesitate to use it with children younger than age eight or nine. Therefore, they use other terms such as learning disability or *reading disabled*. The label is not important. What is important, however, is finding out about what your child can do well, where she or he struggles, and why this struggle is happening. This is the first step in knowing how to help.

Chapter 10

LAWS AND REMEDIATION

How can you help your child? First, you can find out if she or he qualifies for some type of support at school. Each of the English-speaking countries discussed here has its own way of determining which students need help. However, laws tend to change periodically, so you need to check with a local organization (see Appendix I) or your child's school for the most up-to-date information.

In England and Wales, dyslexia is considered a learning difficulty resulting in special educational needs (SEN). Therefore, it is covered by an Education Act and the Special Educational Needs and Disability Act. But as with all the other countries discussed here there is no dyslexia law per se.

Scotland's educational and legal systems are separate from the rest of the UK. It had a new education law go into effect in 2005. Under that law, students unable to benefit from school education without the provision of additional support may be able to access such support. Dyslexia, along with other learning problems, tends to be classified under broad terms such as "specific learning difficulty."

Northern Ireland also has some legislation separate from that found in England and Wales. At the time this book was written, the Special Educational Needs and Disability Order (SENDO) was being drafted.

According to the *International Book of Dyslexia: A Guide to Practice and Resources* (Smyth, Everatt and Salter, 2004), primary level schools in Ireland contain special reading units. There are specific requirements about which students can get help. In 2001, the Task Force on Dyslexia issued a report that could offer "a blueprint for the equitable and effective management of dyslexia in the Irish educational system" (p.132).

Australia does not have a national law that will allow students with dyslexia to get special services. In addition, only a few states (such as New South Wales and Queensland) offer support teachers to students with learning difficulties.

The New Zealand Ministry of Education does not officially recognize dyslexia or any other type of learning disability. Although no law addresses dyslexia, students with dyslexia can qualify for a "reader-writer" for examinations under the New Zealand Qualifications Authority. In addition, some schools allow trained tutors to work with identified students. Teacher education about dyslexia, and learning disabilities in general, is limited.

Canada has no national law that allows students with dyslexia to get help. However, every province has some type of special education law and some students with dyslexia may qualify for special education under the category of learning disability.

The US has a national special education law. Dyslexia is mentioned as one example of a "specific learning disability"; however, it is not a qualifying disability and the diagnosis of dyslexia will not necessarily allow a student access to special education services. Each state must develop its own set of rules to implement and fund the law. In addition, it is up to each local education agency or public school (many private schools are exempt) to interpret and apply those rules and it is up to local taxpayers to approve public school budgets, including (to some extent) special education costs. This system often means that a child eligible for special education in one state or school loses that eligibility if she or he moves. In the US, disabled students not eligible for special education might qualify for protection from discrimination under *Section 504 of the Rehabilitation Act of 1973*. No matter which law is used, students with dyslexia should be able to access *assistive technology* (such as textbooks on tape, reading pens, and speech recognition software).

Regardless of which county you live in, it is doubtful that all students with dyslexia will qualify for special education or remedial help. For example, of the children used as examples in this book (excluding those with deep dyslexia), only Richard and Steven qualified for special education services at their school. The fact that instant help is not always available for their children, and the reality that special education services can legally stop while their children are still working below either their grade level or their potential, can be hard for parents to accept. But schools have to work within both laws and their budgets.

Regardless of the types of services or supports your child receives, she or he will need some accommodations or modifications in school. There is a list of possibilities in Appendix III. You can use that list as a starting point when you talk to your child's teacher(s).

Students with dyslexia need special teaching. It is not enough for them to get the same type of instruction as good readers but at a slower pace. Also, do not be fooled by people who say that they have *the* way to help your child or that they can cure her or his dyslexia. There is more than one way to help people with dyslexia become better readers and spellers. Some methods work for some people but not for others. Also, as far as we know, there is no cure, but there are some things you and the school can do to help. The books, materials, and companies listed in the Appendices I and II might help. In addition, I offer some general ideas below that can be carried out at both home and school. One note of caution though, not every parent is able to teach her or his own child.

If your child has a phonological processing weakness, she or he needs to work on learning about the sounds of language, how to "hear" the sounds in words, and how to make connections between sounds and letters or letter combinations. This is called phonemic awareness and helps children learn phonics. The skills to work on depend on where your child's phonological strengths and weaknesses are.

Some children need to work on skills as simple as rhyming. Reading poems, nursery rhymes, and rhyming books like those by Dr. Seuss, as well as making up rhymes together, can be helpful. Other children need help hearing that spoken words begin with different sounds. So, saying three or four words and having your child tell you the one that begins with a different sound can help. You should start with words whose first sounds can be drawn out (for example, *fast, field, man*) instead of words whose initial phonemes are quick, such as *ball* or *go*. After your child is successful with beginning sounds, you can do the same thing with the last sound in words (for example, *boss, man, goose*).

You can help your child develop better phonological skills by having her or him clap or use objects such as poker chips to show how many words are in spoken sentences, how many syllables are in spoken words, and how many sounds are in spoken words. For example, you might say the sentence "Billy ran down the street" and your child would repeat the sentence, clapping or putting down one chip as she or he says each word.

Some children are helped when an adult says words broken up into sounds and they have to tell what the word is. For example, you might say the sounds /c/-/or/-/n/ and your child would tell you that the word is /corn/. If this is too hard, start with compound words or syllables, like /hot/-/dog/ or

/toa/-/ster/. Alternatively, you might have to break words at the vowel, like /s/-/it/.

You can also ask your child to tell you all the words she or he can think of that begin with a certain sound (not a letter). Teaching your child how to create pig latin words is another way to help because it involves manipulating the sounds of words at a very sophisticated level. (Pig latin is when you take the first sound off a word, move it to the end, and add a long *a*. For example, the word /bike/ becomes /ikebay/, and the word /new/ becomes /oonay/.)

You can also help your child learn to make connections between letters and sounds. Use plastic or other types of "hands-on" letters to spell words and help your child sound them out. This is a good time to introduce the *analogy method*. The analogy method is when you give children clues based on what they already know. For example, if you spell the word *ball*, you could then change the first letter to create new words. So, you might ask, "If this is *ball*, what is this word?" and then change the *b* to a *c*. Then you might ask, "If this is *call*, what is this word?" and change the *c* to an *h*.

People with a weakness in orthographic processing need to learn about spelling patterns, spelling rules, and syllable structures. Giving them verbal and physical cues about how to tell the differences between numbers and letters that look alike can help. Teaching them about *word families* can also be beneficial. Word families are words that share the same spelling pattern and pronunciation, such as *light, might, right, fight*, and so on. This is sometimes called a *linguistic method* for teaching words. It is based on the analogy method since you give children cues based on what they know. For example, "You know how to spell *hill* so how do you think we spell *spill*?"

Drill and practice with irregular words (such as *who, said, what, laugh, move*) and with matching spelling patterns to sounds is not exciting, but can be useful. Therefore, you could make flashcards with spelling patterns like *ate, ow, ough*, and *ph* on them and have your child tell you the sounds they make. You could also say the sounds and have your child write different ways to spell them. For example, if you made the sound /f/, your child could write *f, ff, ph*, and *gh* (as in *tough*). Teach your child about spelling rules, like the silent *e* rule or the fact that one-syllable words with one vowel that end in /f/ usually have two *f*s (such as *buff, cliff, stiff, off*). English spellings are usually predictable, but the spelling system is complex, so you will probably need a good book or a special program to help you.

If your child has an orthographic processing weakness, you can help her or him study spelling by using a *multisensory* approach. In fact, this type of teaching method works with many people with dyslexia regardless of their processing problem(s). A multisensory approach involves using as many different senses as possible. These are usually sight, sound, and touch or movement. So, to study spelling words have your child read the word, copy the word while naming each letter, read the word again and check the spelling, write the word from memory as she or he says each letter, and then repeat the whole process two more times before moving on to the next word.

Teaching children with orthographic processing problems about how words are made is also helpful. For instance, teaching them Greek and Latin roots, prefixes, suffixes, and endings that turn verbs into nouns or nouns into adjectives is beneficial. This increases their vocabulary and helps them with generalized spelling patterns. Also, teaching about the six English syllable structures is a possibility. Again, due to the complexity you will probably need a reference book or a special program for this.

Children who are rate disabled can be helped by re-reading short passages. There are different ways to do this. One way is to pick a book or story that your child can read with at least 98 percent accuracy. The child reads a short part of the book aloud (no more than 100 words), then reads the same part of the book again. This is done three or four times in a row. This gives the child practice at reading familiar words and helps to increase her or his speed. A new passage is read every day, three to five times per week. The whole process should not take more than ten minutes each time. You could also spend a few minutes each day having your child read aloud along with you so she or he gets to know what fluent reading sounds and feels like.

In addition to using books or stories, if your child is rate disabled you should do speeded drills with lists of words. The goal to work toward when doing word list drills is for your child to be able to read each word in one second. You could do a one-minute word list drill every day.

For some rate disabled children, you might need to work on speed drills for letter–sound relationships before you even get to word lists or text reading practice. Other children need to work on recognizing spelling patterns quickly or decoding words rapidly. There are packaged programs and computer software to help with both reading and math fluency. A few examples are listed in Appendix II.

People with dyslexia whose retrieval problems show up in their speech as well as their reading can be helped by activities for improving word retrieval. For example, you could teach lots of different words with similar meanings so if your child cannot think of one there will be others to pick from. You can also teach about words that mean the opposite and develop lists of words based on different kinds of associations. One kind of association work you can do is organizing words into categories. You can then use these categories in retrieval games, such as coming up with a list of things found in a living room or thinking of the different types of animals found in a zoo or used as pets. Learning about root words and affixes can also be helpful. In addition, you can teach your child how to make good use of pauses to recall the word she or he wants, and give her or him practice naming pictures quickly. You might also want to teach your child to keep notebooks with the words she or he needs (such as for science or social studies) so they can be looked up easily. Speech/language pathologists are usually good sources of ideas for how to help children with word retrieval problems.

For any child, you can find out the skills she or he needs to learn for spelling, capitalization, or punctuation by keeping track of errors from a week's worth of assignments. You can then look for patterns, such as errors involving plurals, past tense, homophones, high frequency words, and so on. This will give you a list of skills to work on.

Regardless of his or her age, you definitely should read with your child every day for ten to twenty minutes and talk about the stories as you read them. You should not simply ask yes, no, and fact questions as you read with your child. Instead, ask open-ended questions, such as "Why did so-and-so do that?" or "How do you think so-and-so felt when that happened?" or "What do you think will happen next?" You should also talk about the vocabulary in the story and discuss how the events in the book relate to things your child has done or wants to do, and to the larger world. You can also expand on your child's answers and suggest alternatives.

You should certainly read age-appropriate material to your child. Because children and teenagers with dyslexia cannot read well, they often do not know as much as their friends (remember the Matthew effect?). Reading grade level novels and factual books to your child can help her or him keep up with peers. It is also a good way to spend time together. Again, this should be an interactive process that involves learning new words, discussing ideas, paraphrasing the author's thoughts, and so on.

Having a word bank at home that you review every day is helpful. This can be just a series of index cards with one word on each card. Every week you can chose some words to review in an untimed format. You can keep the cards in a file box and have your child put them away to practice alphabetical order.

All people with dyslexia have trouble making sense out of the way words work. They can have trouble with the sounds, the letters, and the meanings. Therefore, working on all three areas, regardless of your child's processing weaknesses, is beneficial. This allows you to work on improving their weak areas while teaching to their strengths. Consequently, an explicit integrated approach that combines the types of suggestions offered for people with phonological and orthographic dyslexia, and those who are rate disabled might be a good approach to use for everyone.

Obviously, all people with dyslexia will improve if they read as much as possible. Reading, like any other skill, gets better with practice. However, researchers are still trying to discover the best ways to teach people with specific types of reading problems. They are also trying to find out if there are different ways to teach people depending on how old they are, what their reading level is, or what stage of reading development they are at. There is some evidence that the brains of children with processing problems can be retrained so they interpret sounds and letters in more typical ways. But we still have a lot to learn about how to help people with dyslexia.

In addition to accommodations, modifications, special teaching, and academic support at home (and tutoring if necessary), your child might need emotional support. You should monitor her or his emotional well-being and get your child counseling if necessary. And do not forget about yourself, your spouse, and your other children. Any one of you, or even all of you, might need counseling to deal with the many emotional and practical issues that come with a disability.

Having a child with dyslexia can create a tense environment at home. The extra time and effort that goes into homework, coordinating with teachers, attending school meetings, driving to tutoring sessions, and so on put added strain on everyone. Therefore, do not forget to plan fun times for your family on a regular basis. In addition, you might need to deliberately plan one-on-one time with your nondisabled children to be certain they are not accidentally overlooked as you work hard to make sure your child with dyslexia succeeds.

One final comment: there are no medical interventions for dyslexia. There are no pills, shots, operations, and so on that will cure it. There are also no easy solutions. Perhaps as many as one-quarter of adults who were diagnosed with dyslexia as children have been able to improve their word reading and spelling to the point where they will score average on many tests. However, they still tend to be much slower readers than is typical. Therefore, as I mentioned earlier, as far as we know dyslexia is a lifelong condition. On the other hand, new research is calling this opinion into question. It is possible that the proper intervention(s) can retrain children's, or even adults', brains enough for them to overcome their processing differences and develop into average readers and spellers. This is an exciting new area of research. However, it will take a long time to find out if the initial improvements that children show remain with them as they progress into adolescence and adulthood, and if these improvements affect all the different areas impacted by processing weaknesses.

Chapter 11

RETENTION

Retention, being left back, being kept back, staying back – no matter what term is used, the question of whether children with dyslexia should repeat a grade is often raised. After all, if they are not reading or writing on grade level now, how can they hope to succeed next year or the year after that, or the year after that? Under typical circumstances, they cannot. However, these are not typical circumstances.

A child with dyslexia is a child with a processing difference that creates a learning disability. That disability will not go away if she or he spends two years in Grade 1, or Grade 4, or grade whatever. Even if the child did catch up and was on grade level at the end of her or his second year in Grade 2, what is going to happen when she or he falls behind again in Grade 3 or Grade 4? Will the child have to repeat another grade? How many times will she or he have to repeat? How old will the student be when she or he finally graduates from high school?

Researchers have been looking into the effectiveness of retention for a long time and the results have been consistent. On average, staying back does not work, not even for students without disabilities. Although sometimes there is a short-term gain, students who are retained are typically achieving below grade level again within two to three years. Not only that, but students who repeat a grade tend to show increased behavior problems as they get older and are more likely to drop out of school. Repeating just one grade substantially increases the chances that a student will not complete high school, and repeating two grades almost guarantees that the child will drop out.

Research has also shown that retained students are at greater risk for emotional problems, alcohol and drug use, involvement with violence, suicidal thoughts, early sexual activity, and other problems or risky behaviors. Many adults who were kept back as children still remember it as a traumatic event, and in one study children rated being held back as the third most traumatic thing that could happen to them after "losing a parent" and "going blind." Some people argue that retention is better if it happens early, such as in kindergarten. However, the research does not agree with this. The research also does not agree with giving children a "transition" year between kindergarten and Grade 1.

According to the US National Association of School Psychologists (NASP), there can be some benefits to retention. Unfortunately, it is impossible to predict which students will benefit and which will not. However, according to NASP, the effects are less likely to be negative if the child has a positive self-esteem, good relationships with peers, and the necessarily skills that will allow her or him to catch up without difficulty. Also, students who have missed a lot of school due to health problems that have since been straightened out might be helped by repeating a grade. Finally, staying back is more likely to produce a positive result if the child does not simply repeat the same curricula. Instead, the school has to put some kind of interventions in place.

Of course, social promotion (just moving a child through the grades) is not effective either. Schools need to develop alternatives. Unfortunately, this is sometimes impossible due to budget constraints and homeowners being unwilling to see their taxes increase. What they usually do not realize, however, is that the financial costs of keeping a child back and the financial costs that accompany people who drop out of school (such as welfare, unemployment, and jail) are substantially greater than the price tag of changing the way schools work. Investing money to prevent problems is cheaper and easier than trying to fix them after they arise. School boards, governors, legislators, presidents, congress persons, prime ministers, members of parliament, and taxpayers need to be held accountable for creating and paying for programs to help at-risk and failing students.

What are the alternatives to retention for a child with dyslexia? In the US and Canada, if your child qualifies for special education, she or he will be provided with an *individualized education program (IEP)*. This document is developed jointly by educators and parents and specifies the type(s) of help your child will receive. It is supposed to address the individual needs of your child. Therefore, retention will be unnecessary.

In the US, if your child does not qualify for special education but is able to get protection under Section 504, she or he will get a *504 plan*. This document specifies the accommodations and adaptations the school will make to ensure that your child is not discriminated against because of her or his disability. It will also ensure equal access to educational opportunities. As a result, retention will not be needed.

In the US, if your child is unable to get either an IEP or a 504 plan (which should be extremely unlikely), you can work informally with teachers to accomplish the same objectives. There are some examples of the types of accommodations and modifications that your child might need in Appendix III. You can use this list as a starting point regardless of the process used to get help.

Chapter 12

OTHER LEARNING PROBLEMS THAT CAN AFFECT READING

There are other problems in addition to dyslexia that can affect how well people read or understand what they read. A few of these are listed here.

Attention-deficit/hyperactivity disorder (ADHD)

The terms used for attention problems have changed over the years. Currently the term ADHD is used even if the child is not hyperactive. There are three types of attention-deficit/hyperactivity disorder. Some children with ADHD are impulsive and hyperactive but do not have trouble paying attention. Some children are inattentive but are not hyperactive or impulsive. Other children have trouble with both hyperactivity/impulsivity and inattention. Some people with dyslexia also have ADHD. ADHD can cause reading comprehension problems if the person reads too fast or has trouble paying attention to what she or he is reading. Also, people with ADHD often have memory problems, and this makes it hard for them to make connections between ideas or remember what they read.

Hyperlexia

Children with hyperlexia can read words well above their grade level, but struggle to understand what they read. Children with hyperlexia often begin reading words as early as two or three years old. They seem to have a natural grasp for figuring out how written language works. However, even though they can often read fourth or fifth grade books when they are in Grade 1, they struggle to comprehend even age-appropriate materials. Hyperlexia is often linked to *pervasive developmental disorders*, such as autism and Asperger's disorder.

Nonverbal learning disorder/disability (NLD)

There are different types of *nonverbal learning disorders*. Even though the name makes it sound as if children with this problem do not have language difficulties, that is incorrect. Children with NLD can struggle with understanding humor, figurative language, making connections among ideas, and subtle aspects of language. These difficulties can make it hard for them to understand what they read. Although most appear to have no trouble decoding words, some can struggle significantly with learning how to read and are often misdiagnosed with dyslexia. Students with NLD generally do not have trouble remembering the facts about what they read, but can struggle with inferencing, such as reading between the lines.

General and literate language difficulties

Children might not have trouble with any of the processing skills mentioned in this book, but still have a language problem. They might have trouble with vocabulary, grammar, understanding words with multiple meanings, or grasping the way transition words work (such as, *however* or *consequently*). These can make it hard for them to comprehend what they read.

Some children do not have problems with conversational language, but have not had enough exposure to the language of books. This is called literate language and is quite different from the way language is used for talking. If children are unfamiliar with the language styles found in books, they may have trouble with reading comprehension.

Text structure difficulties

All books are written with a certain kind of structure. Novels are narratives and follow what is called story grammar. This is a structure where there is a problem, a reaction to that problem, one or more attempts to solve the problem, an ending, and so on. Textbooks follow other kinds of structures. For example, some are compare–contrast, others are sequential, and still others are problem–solution. Some children have trouble understanding what they read because they do not have a good understanding of text structures.

Chapter 13

A FINAL WORD

You and your child are not alone. There is no firm definition of dyslexia that everyone agrees on, but the estimates are that anywhere from 5 to 20 percent of children have some type of reading disability. A fair estimate might be that, on average, one child in every classroom has some type and degree of dyslexia.

Knowing that your child has a disability is important and provides an explanation for her or his struggles, but it should never be used as an excuse. Dyslexia does not mean that your child does not have to work, study, learn how to write research papers, learn to spell, obey school rules, and so on. It means that she or he needs accommodations and special teaching, but it does not mean that your child can get away with doing anything other than her or his best.

An example I use with children when I discuss their disability with them is that of a broken arm. If a child broke her or his arm, the school would need to make some adjustments. Perhaps someone would have to write for the child while the arm was mending. Similarly, a child with dyslexia will need some adjustments. Perhaps they need to take oral tests instead of written ones. But these adjustments are meant to be temporary. After a broken arm heals, the child needs to work to strengthen it and get it functional again. You would not expect your child to be excused from writing for the rest of her or his time in school simply because she or he once had a broken arm. Likewise, a child with dyslexia needs to work hard to improve her or his reading and writing. As these skills improve, the accommodations and modifications made for them should be adjusted and reduced, and some of them should even be eliminated. Just as with a broken arm, the goal is for your child to become as functional as possible.

Our understanding of dyslexia is constantly changing. We are finding out more about what causes it, how to help people with it, and what the different types of dyslexia are. The information in this book is a beginning, but you might want to find out more. Professional organizations, such as those listed in Appendix I, can help, as can some of the materials found in Appendix II. Finally, your local college library probably has professional journals with articles that will help you know what people are currently researching. There are also articles about dyslexia in mainstream magazines such as *Newsweek* and *Time*. However, regardless of where you look for information you have to be careful because there are some controversial interventions and ideas. The standard advice, "Let the buyer beware," applies to education just as much as it applies to purchasing products or services.

PROFESSIONAL ORGANIZATIONS

US professional organizations

Some of these organizations have branch offices in different regions of the US. The presence of an organization on this list is not intended as either an endorsement or recommendation. While I made every effort to provide accurate contact information, I assume no responsibility for changes that occurred during or after publication.

Council for Exceptional Children
1110 North Glebe Road, Suite 300
Arlington, VA 22201–5704
Phone: (+1) 1–888–CEC–SPED
TTY: (+1) 866–915–5000 (text only)
Fax: (+1) 703–264–9494
www.cec.sped.org

Council for Learning Disabilities
PO Box 4014
Leesburg, VA 20177
Phone: (+1) 571–258–1010
Fax: (+1) 571–258–1011
www.cldinternational.org

International Dyslexia Association
Chester Building, Suite 382
8600 LaSalle Road
Baltimore, MD 21286–2044
Phone: (+1) 410–296–0232
Fax: (+1) 410–321–5069
Voice message requests for information:
1–800–ABCD–123
Email: send emails from website
www.interdys.org

Learning Disabilities Association of America
4156 Library Road
Pittsburgh, PA 15234–1349
Phone: (+1) 412–341–1515
Fax: (+1) 412–344–0224
Email: info@ldaamerica.org
www.ldanatl.org

Recordings for the Blind and Dyslexic (textbooks on tape or CD)
20 Roszel Road
Princeton, NJ 08540
Phone: (+1) 800–221–4792 (membership services)
Email: custserv@rfbd.org
www.rfbd.org

International professional organizations

I found most of the following organizations in the *International Book of Dyslexia: A Guide to Practice and Resources*, edited by Smyth, Everatt, and Salter (2004). I emailed each organization and visited their websites to check on the contact information and made any necessary corrections. The presence of an organization on this list is not intended as either an endorsement or recommendation. While I made every effort to provide accurate contact information, I assume no responsibility for changes that occurred during or after publication.

Australia

Dyslexia-SPELD Foundation WA (Inc)
PO Box 409
South Perth, WA 6951
Phone: (+61) 08–9474–3494
Fax: (+61) 08–9467–1145
Email: support@dyslexia-speld.com
www.dyslexia-speld.com

SPELD NSW Inc
7 Acron Road
St Ives, NSW 2075
Phone: (+61) 02–9144–7977
Fax: (+61) 02–9144–1539
Email: speldnsw@bigpond.com
www.speldnsw.org.au

SPELD Queensland Inc
PO Box 1238
Coorparoo, QLD 4151
Phone: (+61) 07–3394–2566
(1800–671–114 outside metro area)
Fax: (+61) 07–3394–2599
Email: speld@speld.org.au
www.speld.org.au

SPELD South Australia
298 Portrush Road
Kensington, SA 5068
Phone: (+61) 08–8431–1655
Fax: (+61) 08–8364–5751
Email: info@speld-sa.org.au
www.speld-sa.org.au

SPELD (Tas) Inc
Brainworks Resource Centre
250 Murray Street
Hobart, Tasmania 7000
PO Box 154
North Hobart, Tasmania 7002
Phone: (+61) 03–6275–0304; 03–6231–5911
Fax: (+61) 03–6234–3442
Email: speldtasmania@bigpond.com

SPELD Victoria Inc
494 Brunswick Street
North Fitzroy, Victoria 3068
Phone: (+61) 03–9489–4344
Fax: (+61) 03–9486–2437
Email: speldvic@bigpond.com.au
www.speldvic.org.au

Canada

Canadian Council for Exceptional Children
canadian.cec.sped.org

Canadian Dyslexia Association
290 Picton Avenue
Ottawa, Ontario K1Z 8P8
Phone: (+1) 613–722–2699
Fax: (+1) 613–722–7881
Email: info@dyslexiaassociation.ca
www.dyslexiaassociation.ca

see also *International Dyslexia Association* on p.65

Learning Disabilities Association of Canada

323 Chapel Street
Ottawa, Ontario K1N 7Z2
Phone: (+1) 613–238–5721
Fax: (+1) 613–235–5391
Email: information@ldac-taac.ca
www.ldac-taac.ca

England

British Dyslexia Association

98 London Road
Reading, Berkshire RG1 5AU
Phone: (+44) 0118–966–8271
Email: info@dyslexiahelp-bda.demon.co.uk
www.bda-dyslexia.org.uk

Dyslexia Institute

Park House
Wick Road
Egham, Surrey TW20 OHH
Phone: (+44) 01784–222–300
Email: hqreception@dyslexia-inst.org.uk
www.dyslexia-inst.org.uk

Ireland

Dyslexia Association of Ireland

1 Suffolk Street
Dublin 2
Phone: (+353) 1–679–0276
Fax: (+353) 1–679–0273
Email: info@dyslexia.ie
www.dyslexia.ie

New Zealand

Learning & Behaviour Charitable Trust

PO Box 40–161
Upper Hutt
Phone: (+64) 04–567–8781
Fax: (+64) 04–567–8783
www.lbctnz.co.nz

Learning Difficulties Coalition of New Zealand

PO Box 6748
Wellington
Phone: (+64) 04–382–8944
Fax: (+64) 04–382–8943
Email: ldc@paradise.net.nz
www.ldc.co.nz

SPELD NZ

Head Office
PO Box 25
Dargaville
Phone: (+64) 09–439–5955
Email: faj@xtra.co.nz
www.speld.org.nz

Scotland

Dyslexia Scotland

Stirling Business Centre
Wellgreen
Stirling FK8 2DZ
Phone: (+44) 01786–446–650
Fax: (+44) 01786–471–235
Email: info@dyslexiascotland.com
Helpline: helpline@dyslexiascotland.com
www.dyslexiascotland.com

Wales

Bangor Dyslexia Unit
The Dyslexia Unit
University of Wales, Bangor
Bangor, Gwynedd LL57 2DG
Phone: (+44) 01248–382–203
Fax: (+44) 01248–383–614
Email: dyslex-admin@bangor.ac.uk
www.dyslexia.bangor.ac.uk

British Dyslexia Association
98 London Road
Reading, Berkshire RG1 5AU
Phone: (+44) 0118–966–8271
Email: info@dyslexiahelp-bda.demon.co.uk
www.bda-dyslexia.org.uk

Prosiect Dyslecsia Cymru/Welsh Dyslexia Project
Phone: (+44) 01239–682–849
(for support in Welsh and English)
Email: llechryd@btinternet.com
(for support in Welsh);
ian.smythe@ukonline.co.uk
(for assessment questions);
info@actiondyslexia.co.uk
(for teaching questions)
www.welshdyslexia.info

TEACHING AND OTHER RESOURCES

US teaching and other resources
General information
FOR CHILDREN/PRE-TEENS

Farndon, J. (2000) *The Big Book of the Brain: All about the Body's Control Center.* Lincolnwood, IL: Peter Bedrick Books.

If *The Brain* by Seymour Simon does not provide enough information to satisfy your child's curiosity, try this book. It is more detailed about the senses, language, memory, and so on. However, it is still a broad overview. It also does not address reading, dyslexia, or learning problems (although there is a section on mental illness). This book is appropriate for ages 8 to 12. (45 pp.)

Gehret, J. (1996) *The Don't-give-up Kid and Learning Differences*, 2nd edn. Fairport, NY: Verbal Images Press.

A book for Grades 3 and up about learning disabilities in general. Alex wants to be an inventor, but has trouble reading and paying attention. He is tested and gets help in a special classroom with other children who have a variety of learning problems. It includes a Parent Resource Guide. (33 pp.)

Gordon, M.A. (1999) *Let's Talk about Dyslexia*. New York: PowerKids Press.

Designed for children in Grades 1 and 2, this book offers an introduction and overview of what dyslexia is and the kinds of trouble children with dyslexia can have. It encourages children to tell adults if they are having trouble learning to read and spell. (24 pp.)

Hale, N. (2004) *Oh Brother! Growing up with a Special Needs Sibling*. Washington, DC: Magination Press.

This book is designed for children aged 8 to 13. Eleven-year-old Becca is having trouble with her 13-year-old brother, Jonathan. Jonathan has one or more unspecified disabilities. Becca recalls the ups and downs of being Jonathan's sister over the years and of dealing with both the practical and emotional aspects of having a disabled brother. (48 pp.)

Hallowell, E. (2004) *A Walk in the Rain with a Brain*. New York: HarperCollins.

Designed for preschool children and up, this book in verse teaches that everyone has strengths and weaknesses and is smart in different ways. It contains a discussion guide. (32 pp.)

Kressley, C. (2005) *You're Different and That's Super*. New York: Simon & Schuster.

This book for ages four to eight does not directly relate to either dyslexia or learning disabilities, but it has the message that being different is okay. It can be used to open discussions about any type of difference. (64 pp.)

Parker, S. (2004) *The Brain and Nervous System*. Chicago, IL: Raintree.

Like Farndon's *Big Book of the Brain* this book has two pages per topic and is suitable for ages 8 to 12. It is still a broad overview and does not address reading, dyslexia, or learning problems. (48 pp.)

Sanders, P. and Myers, S. (1999) *Dyslexia*. Brookfield, CT: Copper Beech Books.

This book is part of the "What Do You Know About" series and is for Grades 4 and up. Each chapter begins with a one-page introduction to a topic (for example, learning, learning problems, attitudes). That topic is then illustrated in a one- to two-page ongoing comic-book style storyline about some students. Then, aspects of that storyline are discussed on the last page of the chapter. The printed illustrations of what words might look like to a person with dyslexia might not be correct, but otherwise this book is a good introduction. It does not provide much detail, but does touch on topics some other books do not, such as emotional reactions to being a struggling student, resentments siblings can feel, and the bullying that can happen. (32 pp.)

Silverstein, A., Silverstein, V. and Nunn, L. (2001) *Dyslexia*. New York: Franklin Watts.

A good book for students in Grade 3 and up who have dyslexia. It provides facts and an overview without talking down to children. The discussion of processing problems focuses only on phonological dyslexia, but this is a small part of the total book. (48 pp.)

Simon, S. (1999) *The Brain: Our Nervous System*. New York: HarperCollins.

This book has excellent pictures and a clear but broad overview of both the structure and function of the brain. It does not address reading, dyslexia, or learning difficulties, but it is a good place to start if children aged six to ten are interested in the brain. (32 pp.)

Stern, J. and Ben-Ami, U. (1996) *Many Ways to Learn: Young People's Guide to Learning Disabilities*. Washington DC: Magination Press.

Written for children aged 9 to 12, this book explains different types of learning disabilities, discusses intelligence in understandable language, and offers some strategies students can try if they have trouble with reading, math, writing, oral expression, homework, test-taking, or organization. (82 pp.)

FOR TEENS

Donnelly, K. (2000) *Coping with Dyslexia.* New York: Rosen.

This book is written for Grade 8 and up. Despite some of its good points, I do not feel I can recommend it. There are too many incorrect references to what schools are "required" to do or what laws "force" them to do. Also, it begins with the idea that when people with dyslexia read they think in pictures rather than with language. As far I know, this has no basis in research. The book also mentions a controversial theory that dyslexia is caused by an inner ear problem and can be treated medically. (121 pp.)

Farndon, J. (2000) *The Big Book of the Brain: All About the Body's Control Center.* Lincolnwood, IL: Peter Bedrick. (See description p.69)

Moragne, W. (1997) *Dyslexia.* Brookfield, CT: Millbrook Press.

A good book for middle and high school students. It focuses too much on phonological problems, but this does not detract from its overall usefulness. It describes common characteristics and difficulties. Some chapters end with a few ideas for success. It discusses the impact of dyslexia on self-esteem along with relationships with peers and family members. The book contains personal stories of nine teenagers (ages 13 to 18) that help make dyslexia real. This also makes the book useful for adults who want to understand what it is like to have this disability. (96 pp.)

Sanders, P. and Myers, S. (1999) *Dyslexia.* Brookfield, CT: Copper Beech Books. (See description p.70)

Wiltshire, P. (2003) *Dyslexia.* New York: Raintree Steck-Vaugn.

This book packs a great deal of information into its few pages. This can make it a hard read for some children. It contains a lot of details along with hints about helping yourself or someone else who has dyslexia. It is a possible source of information for a child's short research paper on dyslexia. (64 pp.)

Teaching resources

FOR PARENTS AND EDUCATORS

General sources for activity books, workbooks, games, and so on

Academic Communication Associates
PO Box 4279
Oceanside, CA 92052
Phone: (+1) 888–758–9558
www.acadcom.com

Curriculum Associates
PO Box 2001
North Billerica, MA 01862
Phone: (+1) 800–225–0248
www.CAorders.com

Educators Publishing Service
PO Box 9031
Cambridge, MA 02139
Phone: (+1) 800–225–5750
www.epsbooks.com

LinguiSystems
3100 4th Avenue
East Moline, IL 61244
Phone: (+1) 800–766–4332
www.linguisystems.com

York Press Inc.
PO Box 504
Timonium, MD 21094
Phone: (+1) 800–962–2763
www.yorkpress.com

Examples of published programs and materials

This is not intended as an endorsement of any particular programs or materials. These examples are only meant to illustrate the types of resources that are available.

Benchmark Program. Media, PA: Benchmark School ([+1] 610–565–3741), www.benchmarkschool.org

A word identification and vocabulary program that begins with phonemic awareness and progresses to word families and the analogy method for using and understanding orthographic structures. It is suitable for ages five and up. Training is probably necessary before using it.

Concept Phonics, Making Handwriting Flow, Nimble Numeracy, Speed Drills for Arithmetic Facts. Farmington, ME: Oxton House Publishers ([+1] 800–539–READ), www.oxtonhouse.com

Concept Phonics works on automaticity and fluency of decoding, transfer of learning, and memory strategies. It allows teachers to be flexible in how they use it. The program's author is Phyllis E. Fischer and it includes her "reading speed drills" that help develop rapid recognition of both whole words and spelling patterns.

Making Handwriting Flow helps with letter and numeral formation.

Nimble Numeracy and *Speed Drills for Arithmetic Facts* are materials for increasing math fluency.

Corrective Reading. SRA/McGraw-Hill ([+1] 888–772–4543, www.sraonline.com)

These sequenced lessons help older students in need of remedial support develop decoding, comprehension, or both. The program has three levels for decoding and three for comprehension.

Gillingham Manual (and related materials). Cambridge, MA: Educator's Publishing Service ([+1] 800–225–5750, www.epsbooks.com)

A multisensory approach for teaching decoding for both reading and spelling. These materials are suitable for ages five and up and represent the Orton-Gillingham method. Training is required before using it, and teachers need to create many of their own materials.

Great Leaps Reading and *Great Leaps Math.* ([+1] 877–GRLEAPS, www.greatleaps.com)

The reading program focuses on word attack, sight words, and reading fluency. The math program works on math fact fluency and understanding the concepts behind math operations. These materials are suitable for kindergarten to adult.

High Noon Books. Novato, CA: Academic Therapy Publications ([+1] 800–422–7249, www.highnoonbooks.com)

This publisher offers high-interest, low-vocabulary books. These books are designed for older students with reading difficulties. Although the reading level of the books ranges from Grade 1 to Grade 5, the books include topics suitable for ages nine and up, such as mysteries, historical fiction, biographies, science fiction, sports, adventure, science, history, classic literature, and so on.

Instant Spelling Words for Writing. North Billerica, MA: Curriculum Associates ([+1] 800–225–0248, www.CAorders.com)

A series of eight spelling instructional books that focus on the words used in 90 percent of adult writing.

Kidspiration and *Inspiration.* (www.inspiration.com)

Computer software that helps students map, graph, outline, and otherwise visually organize ideas in a variety of ways before they begin writing. *Kidspiration* is for Grades kindergarten to 5. *Inspiration* is for Grades 6 and up.

Let's Read: A Linguistic Reading Program. Cambridge, MA: Educator's Publishing Service ([+1] 800–225–5750, www.epsbooks.com)

A structured, word family approach to teaching reading. It can be used with beginning readers or as a remedial tool at any age.

Lindamood Phoneme Sequencing Program for Reading, Spelling, and Speech (LiPS). Austin, TX: Pro-Ed ([1+] 800–897–3202, www.proedinc.com)

The LiPS program works on bringing phonemic awareness to the conscious level by teaching about how the mouth, lips, and tongue are positioned when making different sounds. It comes in classroom and clinical versions and can be used in the primary grades and up.

Megawords. Cambridge, MA: Educator's Publishing Service ([+1] 800–225–5750, www.epsbooks.com)

A series of books designed for Grade 4 and up. They focus on how to read, spell, and understand multi-syllabic words. The books deal with affixes, roots, spelling and syllable rules, and parts of speech.

QuickReads. Modern Curriculum Press ([+1] 800–526–9907, http://pearsonlearning.com/mcp)

A source for controlled vocabulary, high-interest, nonfiction texts designed to promote reading fluency. The books have reading levels of Grades 2 to 4. More information is available at www.quickreads.org.

Reading Pen II. Wizcom Technologies ([+1] 888–777–0552, www.wizcomtech.com)

This is a self-contained tool that scans and reads back words and phrases. It displays the words as it reads them. It also spells words aloud, gives written definitions, and shows syllable divisions. It cannot read handwriting. It is easy to carry with you.

Reasoning and Writing. SRA/McGraw-Hill ([+1] 888–772–4543, www.sraonline.com)

Designed for Grades kindergarten to 8, this program teaches many aspects of written expression such as story grammar, main idea sentences, paragraphs, poems, descriptive essays, and research papers. In addition, higher level thinking is integrated into the writing activities.

Right into Reading. Cambridge, MA: Educator's Publishing Service ([+1] 800–225–5750, www.epsbooks.com)

These four books provide support in phonemic awareness, letter names, decoding, irregular words, and reading comprehension. Decoding skills are introduced in a slow sequence and appear to cover more ground than *Systematic Sequential Phonics They Use* by Cunningam. In addition to decoding, the books engage students in text reading (fiction, nonfiction, poetry), writing, critical thinking, and vocabulary development. They are designed for use in kindergarten and up.

Self-Directed IEP Kit. Longmont, CO: Sopris West Educational Services ([+1] 800–547–6747, www.sopriswest.com)

This kit consisting of a manual, student workbook, and videos can be used to train students to be more involved in (and even lead) their own IEP meetings. According to the publisher, it can be used with students in Grades 6 to 12 who have learning disabilities, mild to moderate mental retardation, and/or emotional or behavioral problems.

Spellography. Longmont, CO: Sopris West Educational Services ([+1] 800–547–6747, www.sopriswest.com)

A series of three spelling instructional books that cover letter–sound correspondences, spelling patterns, syllable types, irregular words, homophones, and affixes and root words. They also contain activities to work on phonemic awareness, parts of speech, and reading speed. Suitable for remedial work in Grade 6 and up. The publisher recommends users attend a one-day training course.

Touchphonics System. Cambridge, MA: Educator's Publishing Service ([+1] 800–225–5750, www.epsbooks.com)

Hands-on, multisensory materials for teaching decoding and word structure for both reading and spelling. It contains over 200 color-coded plastic letters and letter combinations that, according to the publisher, represent all English letters and letter combinations, such as *ay, ent, ous, str,* and so on. It is suitable for beginning readers, but can also be used as a remedial tool at any age.

Wilson Reading System and *Wilson Fundations.* Oxford, MA: Wilson Language Training ([+1] 508–368–2399, www.wilsonlanguage.com)

These two programs are based on the principles of Orton-Gillingham teaching. They provide multisensory, systematic, and sequential instruction for both reading (decoding) and spelling (encoding). *Fundations* is designed for students in kindergarten through Grade 3. The *Wilson Reading System* is for older students (Grade 3 and up) who are still struggling. According to the publisher, the *Wilson Reading System* is beneficial for students with phonological, orthographic, and/or fluency problems and whose reading or spelling skills are below a Grade 6 level. Unlike the Orton-Gillingham program, Wilson does not require that teachers make their own materials. Teachers should be trained before using the programs.

York Language Decks. Austin, TX: Pro-Ed ([+1] 800–897–3202, www.proedinc.com)

Three sets of 150 cards each that deal with various aspects of English. The cards cover topics such as short vowels, spelling rules, contractions, syllables, Latin roots and affixes, and Greek combining forms. These cards should not be used by themselves. However, they could be used as flashcards or reminders to help students review various spelling rules, sounds, and other aspects of English after they have been taught and practiced in a formal, structured, explicit, and clear manner.

Other instructional resources

This is not intended as an endorsement of any particular books or tools. These examples are only meant to illustrate the types of resources that are available.

Adams, M.J., Footman, B.R., Lundberg, I., and Beeler, T. (1998) *Phonemic Awareness in Young Children: A Classroom Curriculum.* Baltimore, MD: Paul H. Brookes.

This book provides numerous activities that can be done with individual children, small groups, or entire classes to help develop phonemic awareness. The activities are grouped according to the level of phonological awareness involved: listening, rhyming, words and sentences, syllables, initial and final sounds, phonemes, and letters. It also includes an informal assessment tool. Although the title says that the activities are for young children, they can be used with or adapted for students of all ages.

Bear, D.R., Invernizzi, M., Templeton, S., and Johnston, F. (2003) *Words Their Way: Word Study for Phonics, Vocabulary, and Spelling Instruction,* 3rd edn. Upper Saddle River, NJ: Prentice-Hall.

This book offers a good discussion of children's spelling development and provides various informal assessment options designed to discover what stage a child is at. It then offers an in-depth chapter on each developmental stage covering characteristics of that stage, suggested sequences of instruction, and a variety of teaching activities.

Blachman, B.A., Ball, E.W., Black, R., and Tangel, D.M. (2000) *Road to the Code: A Phonological Awareness Program for Young Children.* Baltimore, MD: Paul H. Brookes.

This book offers 44 sequential lessons designed to develop phoneme awareness and letter–sound knowledge for closed syllable words of three phonemes (such as *fat* and *mop*). If a child needs to work on other levels of phonological awareness, such as rhyming or syllable counting, a text such as *Phonemic Awareness in Young Children: A Classroom Curriculum* by Adams *et al.* would be helpful. As with any structured program, the lessons in this book will need to be expanded upon, reviewed, and supplemented.

Cunningham, P.M. (2000) *Systematic Sequential Phonics They Use: For Beginning Readers of All Ages.* Greensboro, NC: Carson-Dellosa Publishing Co.

This book offers a sequence of 140 lessons designed to teach the basics of decoding. The lessons begin with short vowels and then progress through long vowels, vowel pairs, and r-controlled vowels. Along the way, the consonants are also slowly introduced. The later lessons deal with two-letter consonant blends.

Dawson, P. and Guare, R. (2000) *Coaching the ADHD Student.* North Tonawanda, NY: Multi-Health Systems.

A brief guide (31 pp.) designed to help adults learn how to coach upper elementary to college-age students with ADHD. It can be used with any student who needs help with long- and short-term goals, planning, and behavior monitoring. The complete kit comes with some useful monitoring, planning, and goal-setting sheets.

Deshler, D.D., Ellis, E.S., and Lenz, B.K. (1996) *Teaching Adolescents with Learning Disabilities: Strategies and Methods*, 2nd edn. Denver: Love Publishing.

This book is filled with ideas suitable for teaching a variety of learning disabled adolescents including those with dyslexia. It has chapters devoted to reading, writing, math, test-taking and memory, notetaking, social skills, content area learning, and transitioning to college or work.

Hedberg, N.L. and Westby, C.E. (1993) *Analyzing Storytelling Skills: Theory to Practice.* Tucson: Communication Skills Builders.

This comprehensive text covers narrative development, narrative analysis, story grammar analysis, cohesion, and cultural variations in narratives. It offers useful information about how to examine students' writing to discover where they are at in their understanding and use of narrative structure and where they need to go next.

Henry, M.K. (2003) *Unlocking Literacy: Effective Decoding and Spelling Instruction.* Baltimore, MD: Paul H. Brookes.

This text provides information about the structure of English and offers information for teaching students about the orthographic, *morphologic*, and semantic aspects of English. It contains comprehensive lists of spelling rules, syllable types, affixes, Latin roots, and Greek combining forms along with a few sample teaching ideas.

International Dyslexia Association (2002) *Perspectives 28*, 1, Winter.

This edition of the IDA's newsletter was devoted to reading fluency instruction. Its articles contain a variety of ideas suitable for use with children with dyslexia and youth of all ages.

International Dyslexia Association (2004) *Perspectives 30*, 1, Winter.

This edition of the IDA's newsletter was devoted to vocabulary instruction. Its articles contain a variety of ideas suitable for use with children with dyslexia and youth of all ages.

International Dyslexia Association (2005) *Perspectives 31*, 3, Summer.

This edition of the IDA's newsletter was devoted to spelling instruction. The information is suitable for helping children and youth of all ages.

Lambert, L., Rilstone, A., and Wallis, J. (1996) *Once Upon a Time: The Storytelling Card Game.* Roseville, MN: Atlas Games.

A card game designed to help students learn about and practice narrative structure.

Moreau, M.R. and Fidrych, H. (1994) *The Story Grammar Marker.* Springfield, MA: Mindwing Concepts ([+1] 888–228–9746)

This hands-on tool and accompanying manual focus on teaching students about narrative structure. It is suitable for any age and is appropriate for improving reading comprehension, story writing, and oral expression. The publisher also sells products related to other types of text structures.

Richards, R.G. (1999) *The Source for Dyslexia and Dysgraphia*. East Moline, IL: LinguiSystems.

This book is about reading and writing problems. Unfortunately, the dyslexia sections focus only on phonological processing difficulties. It contains a variety of teaching suggestions that can be used at home or in school to help improve a child's phonemic awareness. It is a good complement to *The Source for Reading Fluency* by Swigert.

Richards, R.G. (2003) *The Source for Learning and Memory Strategies*. East Moline, IL: LinguiSystems.

This book describes the brain and memory along with providing chapters devoted to learning facts, reading and spelling, reading comprehension, math, and conceptual learning.

Sedita, J. (2001) *Study Skills: A Landmark School Teaching Guide*, 2nd edn. Prides Crossing, MA: Landmark School.

This text offers suggestions about teaching skills such as organization (notebooks, time, study space), main idea, notetaking, summarizing, using textbooks, studying, test-taking, and report writing.

Swigert, N.B. (2003) *The Source for Reading Fluency*. East Moline, IL: LinguiSystems, Inc.

This book discusses the concept and assessment of reading fluency. It also contains information about remediating problems at the letter, syllable, word, and text levels. It is a good resource and an inexpensive alternative to some of the packaged programs, although it does require teachers and parents to create more of their own materials than the programs do. It is a good compliment to *The Source for Dyslexia and Dysgraphia* by Richards.

A few more resources

Catts, H.W. and Kamhi, A.G. (1999) *Language and Reading Disabilities*. Boston: Allyn & Bacon.

This textbook covers the differences between spoken and written language, stages of reading development, historic and current definitions of reading disabilities, subtypes and causes of reading disabilities, and assessment and intervention issues.

Eurekalert – Science News. www.eurekalert.org

This website is a source for news releases related to a variety of topics. It is one way to find out what researchers are discovering about dyslexia. However, remember that it takes a long time for research to make its way into practice. Studies need to be done and the findings have to be replicated by other people working with different children. Then, these studies need to be redone by still more people so the results can be verified.

Therefore, just because there is a news release about a finding, it does not mean you should expect your child's school to put it into practice. The process of discovering what works and how best to make it work is long and complicated.

International Dyslexia Association. ([+1] 410–296–0232), www.interdys.org

The IDA has a yearly conference with many excellent presenters. However, if you cannot attend, many of the presentations are available on audiotape, usually from Convention Recordings (www.conventionrecordings.com). Not every presentation is worth buying, so it is a hit-or-miss process. Also, when you buy the recordings you do not get the handouts that accompanied the presentations.

Kurnoff, S. (2000) *The Human Side of Dyslexia: 142 Interviews with Real People Telling Real Stories.* Monterey, CA: London Universal Publishing.

This book provides a series of brief summaries based on interviews with parents, siblings, and adults with dyslexia. The individuals with dyslexia appear to have higher than average IQs and many of the parents had extraordinary difficulties with their children's public schools. The book's strength is in the personal side that it offers to the story of dyslexia, especially in Chapter 1 (interviews with parents and siblings) and Chapter 4 (interviews with adults with dyslexia attending college). Additional personal stories about having dyslexia are found in *Dyslexia* by Wendy Moragne (see p.71).

McLeskey, J., Lancaster, M., and Grizzle, K.L. (1995) "Learning disabilities and grade retention: A review of issues with recommendations for practice." *Learning Disabilities Research and Practice 10*, 2, 120–128.

National Association of School Psychologists (1998) "Position statement: Student grade retention and social promotion." Washington, DC: National Association of School Psychologists.

UK teaching resources

The following resources were suggested by various international organizations. This is not intended as an endorsement of any particular program or materials.

General sources

Ann Arbor Publishers Ltd, PO Box 1, Belford, Northumberland NE70 7JX, UK. (+44) 01668–214–460, www.annarbor.co.uk

British Dyslexia Association. Search the website for Literacy Resources to find lists of materials and publishers, www.bda-dyslexia.org.uk

Dyslexia Institute. Explore the Resources Shop section of the website, www.dyslexia-inst.org.uk

LDA, Duke Street, Wisbech, Cambridgeshire PE13 2AE, UK. www.LDAlearning.com

PATOSS, PO Box 10, Evesham, Worcestershire WR11 1ZW, UK.
(+44) 01386–712–650. The website provides a way to order a resource list that contains products which members have found effective, www.patoss-dyslexia.org

Examples of published books and other materials

Cooke, A. (2002) *Tackling Dyslexia: The Bangor Way*, 2nd edn. London: Whurr.

GAMZ Swap and Fix. Worcestershire, UK: GAMZ. ([+44] 01684–562–158, www.gamzuk.com)

Games to practice word recognition; card packs covering vowel spellings, short vowel word patterns, rhymes, soft *c* and *g*, and so on, prefixes, suffixes and rules for affixing. Available as card packs or on CD-ROM.

Hornsby, B. (1998) *Alpha to Omega: The A-Z of Teaching Reading, Writing, and Spelling*, 5th edn. London: Heinemann.

Miles, E. (1998) *The Bangor Dyslexia Teaching System*, 3rd edn. London: Whurr.

Appendix III

EXAMPLES OF CLASSROOM ACCOMMODATIONS AND MODIFICATIONS FOR STUDENTS WITH DYSLEXIA

Spelling, writing, and handwriting

1. Do not penalize students for spelling errors in daily work such as tests (that are not spelling tests), in-class assignments, journal writing, and so on. However, insist on correct spellings in final, edited copies of work.

2. Provide explicit instruction in spelling and the mechanics of writing, but do not let weaknesses in these areas get in the way of instruction in higher level written expression, such as narrative and expository writing.

3. It is important for students and their teachers to understand when and why a piece of writing should be neat. This will release students from the burden of having to make every letter perfect all the time.

4. Allow students to talk with someone before writing. This will help them organize their thoughts before setting them on paper. It may be beneficial to tape record this discussion so the students can refer back to the tape to remind them of what they wanted to say. Outlining, mapping, text frames, and so on could also be developed based upon this conversation.

5. Make sure students can read, and know the meanings of, words they have to learn how to spell.

6. Limit the number of spelling words students have to learn each week.

7. Allow students to produce projects or oral reports rather than written papers.

8. Allow students to dictate answers to an adult or peer as necessary.

9. Provide students with assistive technology for writing, such as speech recognition software, both computer and pocket-sized spellcheckers, and computer programs

that allow them to visually map ideas in various ways. Examples of the latter type of software are *Kidspiration* (Grades kindergarten to 5) and *Inspiration* (Grades 6 and up). These programs help with mapping, outlining, brainstorming, webbing, and diagramming.

10. Provide students with a Franklin spellchecker (www.franklin.com) since it looks for words based on sounds. (Computer spellcheckers look for words based on letters.) A speaking Franklin would be the most beneficial.

11. Allow students to write in their preferred script, either manuscript or cursive.

12. Teach keyboarding skills and allow typed or word-processed work, including homework.

13. Use graphic organizers (e.g., story maps, semantic maps, and text frames) to help students organize their writing before they begin.

14. Because of the students' poor handwriting, let them take spelling tests with moveable letters or a portable word processor such as an Alphasmart (www.alphasmart.com).

15. Allow students to take notes, answer test questions, and so on with a portable word processor such as an Alphasmart or laptop computer.

16. Allow students to dictate homework answers for their parents to write.

Reading

1. Because the students are slow readers, reduce the amount of reading they are required to do. For example, limit how long they spend reading homework to no more than X minutes.

2. Do not ask students to read aloud in mainstream classrooms.

3. Provide students with small-group language arts instruction at their level.

4. Give students any needed help reading tests, worksheets, books, math word problems, and so on.

5. Provide students with assistive technology for reading, such as books on tape or CD, the Reading Pen II from Wizcom Technologies (www.wizcomtech.com), and computer software that will scan text and read it back.

6. Use recorded textbooks from Recordings for the Blind and Dyslexic (www.rfbd.org). Also, contact the local library to inquire about borrowing recorded trade books.

7. Allow students to use a finger, piece of paper, bookmark, or other device to help them keep their place and track while reading.

8. Use an integrated language arts curriculum so the words and skills taught in reading are also the ones being worked on at the same time in writing and spelling.

9. Tape record test questions so students can listen to them through headphones while taking the test.

10. All written materials such as tests and handouts should be in at least 12-point font and double-spaced so students can read and track more easily.

11. Do not use fluency/speed as the basis for placement in reading material since this can lead to boredom. Instead, use reading level appropriate material coupled with specific instruction designed to improve fluency.

Math

1. Teach math through conceptual understanding and not just through facts and procedures.

2. Allow students to use a calculator for math and content area computations. Do not let their computational weaknesses or trouble with math fact memorization prevent them from being taught higher level skills.

3. Avoid timed or speeded math tests.

4. If the students' weak memory continues to be an obstacle to their ability to perform math operations, they would benefit from having a book with models of math problems to which they can refer as a reminder of the procedures involved in solving various types of problems. Another possibility is the use of self-monitoring sheets which list the important steps involved in specific multi-step computations. The students can use these sheets as checklists to aid them in written calculations. Similar self-monitoring sheets can be used for math problem solving.

5. Include calculator skills in students' math programs.

6. Use enlarged copies of math book pages so students can write answers directly on the paper and not have to copy problems. If this is not possible and if the students copy a problem wrong but compute the correct solution to the problem they wrote down, count the problem as correct.

7. Allow students to use math fact charts and other reference sheets as a memory aid.

Copying

1. Teachers should carefully consider whether the act of copying is important to the task being taught or measured. If it is not, use photocopied book pages, consumable texts, copied notes from the board, and so on. This will assist students in getting work done better and faster.

2. Reduce or eliminate copying requirements.

3. Use enlarged copies of textbook pages so students can write answers directly on the paper and not have to copy.

4. Whatever students need to copy should be written in manuscript.

5. Do not require students to copy what they cannot read.

Notetaking

1. Due to their poor spelling and handwriting, provide students with pre-written copies of notes, overheads, and so on.

2. Allow students to focus on listening rather than having them both listen and take notes. Two possible ways to do this are by providing them with copies of teacher notes and by giving them partially completed advance organizers (such as outlines).

3. Allow students to tape record lectures.

4. Allow students to use a laptop computer or portable word processor (such as an Alphasmart, www.alphasmart.com) in class for notetaking.

5. Assign a peer the task of taking notes for the students. Use a photocopy machine to create the extra sets of notes.

6. Present information at a pace that matches the students' verbal processing speed, repeat important information, verbally mark important information (e.g., "This next part is very important."), and use visual aids instead of pure lecture.

7. Teachers should use only manuscript writing on the board, overhead, handouts, and so on.

Grading and assessment

1. Grade students' work on the content of the class (e.g., science) and not on spelling or the mechanics of written expression.

2. Because of the students' word finding problems, they would benefit from taking recognition rather than recall tests. Recognition tests include matching, multiple choice, and fill-ins (when the words to be used are supplied).

3. The students will be able to explain the gist of what was studied, but be unlikely to recall specific vocabulary, dates, and other exact details. Therefore, grade them based on the gist.

4. Allow students to display their knowledge orally, such as with oral tests and reports, or visually, such as with projects.

5. Allow students to back up written responses with verbal answers whenever their answers are not readable or otherwise in doubt. Grades should be based on the verbal responses.

6. Give students extra help reading tests, quizzes, and so on.

7. Give students extra time to complete tests or reduce the length of tests so they can be completed within regular class periods.

8. Avoid timed tests.

9. Score tests (especially timed ones, if they are necessary) according to the number correct out of the number attempted.

10. Allow students to dictate answers, including test answers, to an adult or peer as appropriate.

11. Allow students to take oral tests. If they are uncomfortable not taking a test with the rest of the class, let them take the regular test but grade only the oral exam.

12. Give students partial credit in math when their reasoning is correct but their computation is wrong (unless they had access to a calculator).

13. Homework should be graded based on the amount completed in X amount of time.

14. Use adapted tests, such as multiple choice instead of essay, and/or a fewer number of questions.

15. Grade students' work based on effort and not just skill attainment.

16. Supply students with a list of the content area vocabulary words to which they can refer while taking tests, such as essay tests.

17. Allow students to take tests on a computer so the questions can be read to them and/or they can type or dictate answers rather than write them.

18. Use regular, short quizzes instead of infrequent, large tests.

19. Tape record test questions so students can listen to them through headphones while taking tests.

20. Because of the students' trouble tracking across lines of print, use at least a 12-point simple font and double-spacing.

21. Allow students to write directly on tests, avoid computer scannable sheets.

22. Tell students what test formats will be (e.g., multiple-choice, essay, etc.) so they will know how to study for them.

23. Allow students to take tests in an alternative setting where noise and/or other distractions are reduced.

24. Allow students to type test answers on an Alphasmart (www.alphasmart.com) or laptop computer.

Homework

1. Homework should be graded based on the amount completed in X amount of time.

2. Provide peer and/or adult support for students at home as they complete assignments.

3. Allow students to dictate homework answers to their parent(s).

4. Allow typed homework assignments.

5. Because the students are slow readers, reduce the amount of reading they are required to do. For example, limit how long they spend reading homework.

Memory

1. Keep oral directions short and check with students to be sure they remember what to do and how to do it.

2. Provide written directions to accompany oral ones.

3. Have students repeat directions back and/or paraphrase them before beginning independent work.

4. Students should use assignment books to record homework, test dates, and so on. The books can also be used as places to record short-term goals toward the completion of long-term assignments.

5. Provide students with advance organizers.

6. Reinforce verbal directions with visual cues. For example, list homework assignments on the board and read them to students instead of just saying them and having students write from memory.

7. Provide review, over-learning, and repetition.

8. Reduce the amount of information students have to memorize.

9. Provide visual and/or hands-on material to accompany lectures.

10. Use regular, short quizzes instead of infrequent large tests.

Retrieval

1. Allow students extra processing time when they have to answer questions and/or follow directions.

2. Direct questions to the class as a whole, pause to allow students to process the questions and formulate replies, then call on them.

3. Because of the students' word finding problems, they would benefit from recognition rather than recall tests. Recognition tests include matching, multiple choice, and fill-ins (when the words to be used are supplied). In addition, students might be able to explain the gist of what was studied, but be unable to recall specific vocabulary, dates, and so on. Therefore, grade them based on the gist.

4. Supply students with lists of content area vocabulary to which they can refer while taking tests, such as essay tests.

5. Allow students to use math fact charts and other reference sheets due to their poor memory.

Speed

1. Give students more time for work completion and/or reduce their workload. Look for quality rather than quantity.

2. Allow students extra time to perform tasks.

3. Do not use timed tests.

4. Shorten assignments so they can be completed in a reasonable amount of time.

5. Score tests (especially timed ones if they are necessary) according to the number correct out of the number attempted.

6. Due to the students' slower rate of auditory processing, put all instructions and homework assignments on the board. Also, provide copies of written notes or provide students with partially completed graphic organizers at the beginning of class.

Attention-deficit/hyperactivity disorder (ADHD)

1. Seat students in the least distracting location in the classroom but near the point of instruction.

2. Help students get started with individual seatwork. Have them repeat the directions quietly to the teacher. Check back periodically to see if they are still on track.

3. Break assignments into smaller parts.

4. Do not expect students to work independently for longer than their attention spans allow. Check in with them regularly to see how they are doing and to help keep them on task.

5. Give students extra time to work on assignments and tests, or reduce the length of the work so it can be completed within regular class periods.

6. Help students develop a series of short-term goals with specific completion dates for the achievement of long-term assignments.

7. Do not take away recess as a punishment for misbehavior or use recess as a time for students to get caught up on work.

8. Give regular feedback and praise success. Reward more than you punish. Praise should specify the appropriate behavior being reinforced and be delivered as soon as possible after it occurs.

9. Coordinate behavioral goals with parents and other professionals who are working with the students.

10. Give only one task at a time. Provide movement breaks between tasks.

11. When testing, make sure you are evaluating knowledge and not attention span.

12. Keep rules and instructions clear and brief, and accompany them with written or pictured reminders.

13. Deliver consequences quickly, if not immediately, along with a verbal explanation of what students did and why it was incorrect. However, do not engage in a discussion with the students. Work on changing only one or two misbehaviors at a time.

14. Change or rotate reinforcers or rewards regularly (for example, every two to three weeks).

15. Anticipate problems during transitions or known difficult times. Remind students of the behavior rules for the situation, have them repeat them back to you, and remind them of what the rewards or consequences will be.

16. Use a predictable classroom structure and routine. Keep rules short and post them where students can easily see them. Tell students of any changes in routine before they happen.

17. Use daily or weekly behavior report cards to keep parents informed and to coordinate behavior programs between home and school.

18. Provide students with a second set of textbooks to keep at home.

19. Provide students with a coordinator or organizational coach. This person would make sure assignment books are filled out, homework supplies are in the students' bookbags, homework is handed in, lockers are kept neat, and so on. They would also help students set short- and long-term goals, check on progress toward those

goals, give study hints and teach study skills, help problem solve, identify supports, and so on.

20. Grade students' homework based on what is accomplished in X amount of time.

21. Provide students with the external structure they lack internally. For example, give them lists and a color-coded binder. Teach them how to be organized. Do not assume that by simply providing students with the tools to be organized they will "take to" them and/or know how to use them. Organization is a skill that needs to be taught, and people can take a long time to learn it.

22. Provide graphic organizers at the beginning of lessons and to accompany homework.

23. Provide physical breaks during the school day so students can get up and expend energy.

24. Provide students with a portable study carrel in each classroom as needed.

25. Do not assign more than one long-term project at a time.

26. Provide as many hands-on teaching and learning experiences as possible.

27. Provide students with a fidget toy such as a Tangle or Koosh ball and/or allow them to draw or doodle during class, such as during lectures. Such hands-on work can help some students focus their attention.

28. Keep extra supplies, such as pencils, on hand in each classroom.

29. Allow students to focus on listening rather than having them both listen and take notes. Two possible ways to do this are by providing them with copies of teacher notes and by giving them partially completed advance organizers (such as outlines).

30. Use regular, short quizzes instead of infrequent large tests.

31. Allow students to write directly on tests.

32. Allow students to take tests and do work in alternative settings where noise and/or other distractions are reduced.

33. Do not call on students in class unless it is clear they have been actively paying attention.

34. Allow students to listen to music as they work, such as with a portable radio or CD player and headphones. This helps some students focus their attention.

General

1. Make use of the students' reasoning strengths by teaching the logic behind the facts. Teach for understanding and not just memorization.

2. Pre-teach vocabulary and provide the necessary background information before beginning lessons. Help students access their pre-existing knowledge base. Pre-teaching activities such as brainstorming, semantic mapping, and so on are helpful. Relate new information to previously acquired knowledge.

3. Allow students to write in schoolbooks with erasable highlighters. Alternatively, encourage students to write on sticky notes and then put the notes in the appropriate places in textbooks to mark important concepts, summarize key points, keep track of vocabulary, and so on.

4. Provide students with an extra set of schoolbooks to keep at home.

GLOSSARY

acquired dyslexia A reading problem that develops after some type of brain injury. See also **dyslexia**.

analogy method A way of helping children make connections between a new word or skill and what they already know. For example, teaching them how to read or spell a word they do not know, such as *stood*, by referring to a word they already know that has the same spelling pattern and pronunciation, such as *good*.

assistive technology Any equipment or product that helps to maintain or improve the functional skills of a disabled child.

decode and **decoding** See **word attack**.

deep dyslexia A very rare reading problem where people make errors by substituting words from the same class, such as reading *hop* for *walk*, or *snowmobile* for *car*. These mistakes have to occur often when people read words in an untimed list and not just when they read text.

developmental delay A delay in a child's acquisition of one or more skills. This delay does not necessarily mean that the child has a disability. It may simply mean that she or he is learning some skill(s) at a slower than average pace. Developmental delays are not usually talked about after a child turns eight or nine years old. If there is still a problem after those ages, it is usually assumed to be because of some type of disorder or disability.

developmental dyslexia A reading problem that is present from an early age without any brain injury. See also **dyslexia**.

dysfluent The opposite of fluent. Reading fluency refers to more than just reading speed, although that is what many people think of when they hear the term mentioned. Reading fluency has to do with someone's ability to read quickly, accurately, expressively, and to make use of phrasing, intonation, and rhythm. The complex nature of reading fluency makes it hard to measure, which is why most "fluency" tests only examine reading speed. Although having a good reading speed does not guarantee that someone will read fluently, it is not possible to read fluently without having a good reading speed. Reading fluency is an important bridge between reading the words correctly and understanding what you read. Having a good reading speed allows readers the opportunity to recognize and decode words while at the same time attending to comprehension.

dysgraphia A problem with the physical act of writing. It is not just trouble putting ideas into written words. It is not just poor spelling or bad grammar. It is also not just messy handwriting. Dysgraphia is a struggle with using a pen or pencil to copy and write letters, or even to draw simple shapes or lines.

dyseidetic dyslexia See **orthographic dyslexia**.

dyslexia Significant trouble reading words because of one or more **processing** problems. It can also affect spelling and other skills. Dyslexia is not due to laziness, mental retardation, inadequate teaching, emotional difficulties, poor vision or hearing, and so on. See also **deep dyslexia**, **mixed dyslexia**, **orthographic dyslexia**, **phonological dyslexia**, **rapid naming**, **rate disabled**, **retrieval problems**.

dysphonetic dyslexia See **phonological dyslexia**.

executive functions A variety of skills that have to do with directing and controlling yourself in different ways. Examples of executive functions are shifting behaviors, inhibiting behaviors, planning, organizing, strategizing, selectively attending, flexibility, emotional regulation, and working memory. Executive functions are, in part, the abilities that allow us to use our intelligence. For example, no matter how smart someone is, if they are impulsive and therefore have trouble stopping to think before they act (that is, they have trouble inhibiting actions), they are unlikely to behave at times in a manner that reflects their intellectual level.

504 plan In the US, this is a plan that spells out the accommodations and related services a student will receive to ensure she or he has access to academic and nonacademic programs and activities. The law does not require schools to involve parents in writing the plan. A disabled student who does not qualify for special education services might be able to obtain protection from discrimination under a 504 plan.

function words "Small" words like *but*, *the*, *through*, *is*. They are adverbs, articles, prepositions, auxiliary verbs, and conjunctions.

homophones Two or more words that are pronounced the same but that have different meanings and often different spellings, such as *by* and *buy* , *sale* and *sail*, and *two*, *to*, and *too*.

individualized education program (IEP) A written document developed for each student in special education. In the US, it lists the student's present levels of performance and identifies the skills to be worked on and the expected amount of growth for a given year. It also states how often and where services will be provided, who will provide them, and lists the accommodations and modifications the student will receive to be successful in mainstream classrooms. Each student's IEP has to be updated at least yearly, although a 2004 federal law allows for some multi-year IEPs. An IEP is a guarantee of services, but it is not a guarantee of growth. The levels listed as expected annual progress are simply best guesses. Parents are legally part of teams that develops IEPs.

IQ, IQ test The idea that someone's intelligence can be summarized by a number (an IQ score) has been around for a long time. It is not a very practical notion since intelligence is complex and no one's brain can be reduced to a number. IQ tests measure different cognitive skills, such as verbal memory, visual perception, spatial skills, speed of work completion, and higher-level reasoning. Different tests measure different combinations of skills. As a result, different IQ tests can produce different IQ scores for the same person.

learning disability A condition that makes learning hard. It is caused by some type of **processing** problem and cannot be due to **developmental delay**, mental retardation, inadequate teaching, emotional disturbance, physical problems such as poor eyesight, or other difficulties.

linguistic method A way of teaching reading that focuses on teaching about **word families**. "The fat cat sat on the mat" is a sentence that might appear in an easy linguistic reading book.

long-term memory Information stored in your brain that you can recall as needed.

mixed dyslexia Reading problems caused by more than one type of processing difficulty. See also **dyslexia, orthographic dyslexia, phonological dyslexia, rapid naming, rate disabled, retrieval problems**.

morphemes The smallest parts of language that carry meaning. The word *break* is a morpheme. The word *breakable* has two morphemes (the root word *break* and the suffix *–able*, which means *capable*). The word *unbreakable* has three morphemes (the root word *break*, the suffix *–able*, and the prefix *un–*, which means *opposite*). The word *talked* has two morphemes (the root word *talk* and the inflected ending *–ed*, which shows past tense).

morphologic Having to do with **morphemes**.

multisensory A way of teaching that uses the simultaneous combination of sight, sound, and movement or touch to work on the same skill.

nonverbal learning disorder/disability Various types of learning problems that are associated with significant weaknesses in **visual perception** and **spatial skills**. They can affect organization, math development, word decoding, reading comprehension, social understanding, written expression, and some aspects of oral language.

orthography The spelling and writing systems of a language. English orthography includes the 26 letters of the alphabet along with letter combinations (e.g., *th*, *ough*), irregular words (e.g., *the*) and written numerals.

orthographic dyslexia A type of reading problem where people have trouble remembering how letters and words look. It is sometimes called **surface dyslexia** or **dyseidetic dyslexia**. See also **dyslexia**.

orthographic processing The abilities to recognize and remember numerals, letters, letter combinations, and words. See also **visual perception** and **processing**.

pervasive developmental disorders (PDD) These disorders are characterized by severe problems with language development and reciprocal social skills. Children with PDD often have stereotypical behaviors. These are repetitive, nonfunctional motor movements, such as hand flapping, spinning, or self-biting. Pervasive developmental disorders show up early in children's lives and affect their ability to connect to the world and people. Children with PDD often appear to be marching to their own drummers. In the US, PDD includes autism, Asperger's disorder, Rhett's syndrome, childhood disintegrative disorder, and pervasive developmental disorder not otherwise specified.

phonemes The individual sounds that make up words. The word *cat* has three phonemes – /c/ /a/ /t/. Phonemes are not the same as letters. The word *fought* has six letters but only three phonemes – /f/ /o/ /t/. (When letters are placed inside slash marks, it refers to their sounds and not their written form.)

phonemic awareness The abilities to "hear," think about, and manipulate the individual sounds in words. It is a type of **phonological processing**.

phonics Learning about the connections between sounds and letters. See also **word attack**.

phonological dyslexia A type of reading problem where people have trouble making sense out of speech sounds and their connections to letters, sometimes called **dysphonetic dyslexia**. See also **dyslexia**.

phonological processing The abilities to interpret speech sounds correctly, remember what you hear, identify the sounds in words, and reproduce speech sounds properly.

phonology The sound system of a language.

processing Things your brain does to make sense out of, interpret and understand, integrate, and retain and recall what you see, hear, feel, smell, taste, remember, and so on. Basically, almost anything your brain is involved in, other than automatic actions like breathing, includes one or more types of processing. See also **orthographic processing, phonological processing, rapid naming, retrieval problems**.

rapid naming How quickly people can name simple learned objects or symbols that they are looking at, such as letters, numbers, or colors. It is a complex skill that involves at least the abilities to quickly and consistently locate and retrieve specific information from **long-term memory** when you need it and apply a verbal label to that information. Problems with rapid naming can be associated with slow reading speed, **retrieval problems**, and weak recognition of irregular words and homophones.

rate disabled People who are very slow readers in comparison to their intelligence and reading levels. All types of **dyslexia** have the ability to produce slow reading, but some dyslexics only have a problem with reading speed.

reading disabled A general term for people who have trouble reading as well as they should.

retrieval problems Difficulty getting information out of **long-term memory**. The "tip of the tongue" experience is a type of retrieval problem.

Section 504 of the Rehabilitation Act of 1973 A US law that requires schools receiving federal money to accommodate some students with disabilities and give them equal access to education and services.

semantic The meaning of words or language.

sight words Words that people can read without sounding them out because of repeated practice with them; also called *sight vocabulary*.

spatial skills The abilities to see or visualize how things are arranged in space and to know where you are in relation to other things. People with poor spatial skills might bump into things a lot, be unable to write numbers or letters in straight columns, and might not put consistent spaces between letters and words when writing.

special education Individualized education provided to some disabled children. In the US, it involves changes in what children are taught, how children are taught, and/or where children are taught based on their individual needs. Special education must be provided according to both federal laws and state regulations. Most states require that students in special education receive *an* appropriate education. It does not have to be the most appropriate education, the best education, or provide maximum benefit to the child.

story grammar The organizational structure of narratives. Stories from a western European background usually involve a character facing some problem in a specific time and place. The character then responds to that problem, comes up with one or more ways to solve it, and attempts each of those solutions until one works. Along the way, new obstacles may crop up that produce new responses and solutions. Finally, all the problems are solved. Stories also include various emotional reactions.

surface dyslexia see **orthographic dyslexia**.

verbal memory The ability to remember what people say. It is a kind of auditory memory and is part of **phonological processing**.

visual perception This does not refer to how well people can see but to how well their "mind's eye" works. It includes developing mental pictures and then remembering and using those pictures. **Orthographic processing** is one type of visual perception. People with **orthographic dyslexia** do not have trouble with all aspects of visual perception. Their difficulty is usually limited to the storage, interpretation, and/or memory of symbols such as letters and numbers.

word attack The ability to sound out unknown words. To do this people have to be able to segment printed words into chunks, know what sounds to give these chunks, and then blend the parts together to result in real words that can be pronounced as wholes.

word families Words that share a common spelling pattern and pronunciation, such as *men*, *hen*, and *pen*.

BIBLIOGRAPHY

Ackerman, P.T., Holloway, C.A., Youngdahl, P.L., and Dykman, R.A. (2001) "The double-deficit theory of reading disability does not fit all." *Learning Disabilities Research and Practice 16*, 3, 152–160.

Adams, M.J. (1990) *Beginning to Read: Thinking and Learning about Print.* Cambridge, MA: MIT.

American Psychiatric Association (2000) *Diagnostic and Statistical Manual of Mental Disorders*, 4th edn, text revision. Washington, DC: American Psychiatric Association.

Attwood, T. (1998) *Asperger's Syndrome: A Guide for Parents and Professionals.* Philadelphia: Jessica Kingsley Publishers.

Badian, N.A. (1997) "Dyslexia and the double deficit hypothesis." *Annals of Dyslexia 47*, 69–87.

Barker, T.A., Torgesen, J.K., and Wagner, R.K. (1992) "The role of orthographic processing skills on five different reading tasks." *Reading Research Quarterly 27*, 4, 334–345.

Barkley, R.A. (1998) *Attention-Deficit Hyperactivity Disorder: A Handbook for Diagnosis and Treatment*, 2nd edn. New York: Guilford Press.

Bate, S. and Felton, R. (2001) *Research to Practice: Coaching Reading Fluency.* Paper presented at the meeting of the International Dyslexia Association, Albuquerque, NM, October.

Berninger, V.W. (1990) "Multiple orthographic codes: Key to alternative instructional methodologies for developing the orthographic-phonological connections underlying word identification." *School Psychology Review 19*, 4, 518–533.

Canter, A., Carey, K., and Dawson, P. (1998) *Retention and Promotion: A Handout for Teachers.* Washington, DC: National Association of School Psychologists, June.

Catts, H.W. and Kamhi, A.G. (2005) *Language and Reading Disabilities,* 2nd edn. Boston: Allyn & Bacon.

Cavey, D.W. (2000) *Dysgraphia: Why Johnny Can't Write. A Handbook for Teachers and Parents.* Austin, TX: Pro-Ed.

Coltheart, M., Masterson, J., Byng, S., Prior, M., and Riddoch, J. (1983) "Surface dyslexia." *Quarterly Journal of Experimental Psychology 35A*, 3, 469–495.

Dawson, P. (1998) "A primer on student grade retention: What the research says." *Communique 26*, 8 June, 28–30.

Deshler, D.D., Ellis, E.S., and Lenz, B.K. (1996) *Teaching Adolescents with Learning Disabilities: Strategies and Methods*, 2nd edn. Denver: Love Publishing.

Dyslexics not doomed to life of reading difficulties (2004, February 12). Retrieved from http://www.eurekalert.org/pub_releases/2004-02/uow-dnd020904.php.

Ehri, L.C., Nunes, S.R., Stahl, S.A., and Willows, D.M. (2001a) "Systematic phonics instruction helps students learn to read: Evidence from the national reading panel's meta-analysis." *Review of Educational Research 71*, 3, 393–447.

Ehri, L.C., Nunes, S.R., Willows, D.M., Schuster, B., Yaghoub-Zadeh, Z., and Shanahan, T. (2001b) "Phonemic awareness instruction helps children learn to read: Evidence from the national reading panel's meta-analysis." *Reading Research Quarterly 36*, 3, 250–287.

Ellis, A.W. (1993) *Reading, Writing and Dyslexia: A Cognitive Analysis*. Hillsdale, NJ: Lawrence Erlbaum Associates, Inc.

ERIC (Clearinghouse on Disabilities and Gifted Education) (2001) *Educating Exceptional Children: A Statistical Profile*. Arlington, VA: Council for Exceptional Children, April.

Flanagan, D.P., Genshaft, J.L., and Harrison, P.L. (1997) *Contemporary Intellectual Assessment: Theories, Tests, and Issues*. New York: Guilford Press.

Gardner, H. (1983) *Frames of Mind*. New York: Basic Books.

Gilger, J.W. (2003) "Genes and dyslexia." *Perspectives 29*, Spring, 6–8.

Gilger, J.W. (2004) "The promise and practical applications of genetic research on dyslexia." *Perspectives 30*, Summer, 30–33.

Goleman, D. (1995) *Emotional Intelligence*. New York: Bantam.

Hanley, J.R., Hastie, K., and Kay, J. (1992) "Developmental surface dyslexia and dysgraphia: An orthographic processing impairment." *Quarterly Journal of Experimental Psychology 44A*, 2, 285–319.

Hultquist, A.M. (1996) "Orthographic processing in reading disabled students and reading age controls: Whole word and subword units." Doctoral dissertation, American International College.

Hultquist, A.M. (1997) "Orthographic processing abilities of adolescents with dyslexia." *Annals of Dyslexia 47*, 89–114.

Jenkins, J.R., Fuchs, L.S., van den Broek, P., Espin, C., and Deno, S.L. (2003) "Sources of individual differences in reading comprehension and reading fluency." *Journal of Educational Psychology 95*, 4, 719–729.

Johnson, D.J. and Myklebust, H.R. (1967) *Learning Disabilities: Educational Principles and Practices*. New York: Grune & Stratton.

Kuhn, M.R. and Stahl, S.A. (2003) "Fluency: A review of developmental and remedial practices." *Journal of Educational Psychology 95*, 1, 3–21.

Kurnoff, S. (2000) *The Human Side of Dyslexia: 142 Interviews with Real People Telling Real Stories*. Monterey, CA: London Universal Publishing.

Lefly, D.L. and Pennington, B. F. (1991) "Spelling errors and reading fluency in compensated adult dyslexics." *Annals of Dyslexia 41*, 143–161.

Livingstone, M.S., Rosen, G.D., Drislane, F.W., and Galaburda, A.M. (1991) "Physiological and anatomical evidence for a magnocelluar defect in developmental dyslexia." *Proceedings of the National Academy of Science USA 88*, 18, 7943–7947.

Lyon, G.R. and Chhabra, V. (1996) "The current state of science and the future of specific reading disability." *Mental Retardation and Developmental Disabilities 2*, 1, 2–9.

McBride, G.M., Dumont, R., and Willis, J.O. (2004) "Response to response to intervention legislation: The future of school psychologists." *School Psychologist 58*, Summer, 86–91, 93.

McLesky, J., Lancaster, M., and Grizzle, K. (1995) "Learning disabilities and grade retention: A review of issues with recommendations for practice." *Learning Disabilities Research and Practice 10*, 2, 120–128.

McNulty, M.A. (2003). "Dyslexia and the life course." *Journal of Learning Disabilities 36*, 4, 363–381.

Manis, F.R., Szeszulski, P.A., Holt, L.K., and Graves, K. (1988) "A developmental perspective on dyslexic subtypes." *Annals of Dyslexia 38*, 139–153.

Murphy, L. and Pollatsek, A. (1994) "Developmental dyslexia: Heterogeneity without discrete subgroups." *Annals of Dyslexia 44*, 2, 120–146.

National Association of School Psychologists (1998) "Position statement: Student grade retention and social promotion." Washington, DC: National Association of School Psychologists, June.

Neisser, U., Boodoo, G., Bouchard, T.J., Boykin, A.W., Brody, N., Ceci, S.J., *et al.* (1996) "Intelligence: Knowns and unknowns." *American Psychologist 51*, 2, 77–101.

Newby, R.F., Recht, D.R. and Caldwell, J. (1993) "Validation for a clinical method for the diagnosis of two subtypes of dyslexia." *Journal of Psychoeducational Assessment 11*, 72–83.

Olson, R.K. (2004) "Genes, environment, and the components of the reading process." *Perspectives 30*, Summer, 6–9.

Olson, R., Wise, B., Conners, F., Rack, J., and Fulker, D. (1989) "Specific deficits in component reading and language skills: Genetic and environmental influences." *Journal of Learning Disabilities 22*, 6, 339–348.

Pennington, B.F. (1991) *Diagnosing Learning Disorders: A Neuropsychological Framework.* New York: Guilford Press.

Quinn, B. and Malone, A. (2000) *Pervasive Developmental Disorder: An Altered Perspective.* London: Jessica Kingsley Publishers.

Ranby, M.J. and Swanson, H.L. (2003) "Reading comprehension skills of young adults with childhood diagnoses of dyslexia." *Journal of Learning Disabilities 36*, 6, 538–555.

Rawson, M.B. (1995) *Dyslexia over the Lifespan: A Fifty-five Year Longitudinal Study.* Cambridge, MA: Educators Publishing Service.

Richardson, S.O. and Sherman, G.F. (1994) *Doctors Ask Questions about Dyslexia: A Review of Medical Research*, 2nd edn. Baltimore: International Dyslexia Association.

Roberts, R. and Mather, N. (1997) "Orthographic dyslexia: The neglected subtype." *Learning Disabilities Research and Practice 12*, 4, 236–250.

Ryan, M. (2004) "Social and emotional problems related to dyslexia." *Perspectives 30*, Spring, 1–4.

Shaywitz, S.E. (1996) "Dyslexia." *Scientific American*, November, 98–104.

Siegel, L.S. (1985) "Deep dyslexia in childhood?" *Brain and Language 26*, 1, 16–27.

Smith, D.R. (2004, January 21–23) "Making the reading connection." Retrieved 2 August 2004 from Harcourt Assessment website: http://harcourtassessment.com/hai/Images/resource/library/pdf/WISC-IV_and_Reading_Handout.pdf

Smyth, I., Everatt, J., and Salter, R. (eds) (2004) *International Book of Dyslexia: A Guide to Practice and Resources.* Chichester: Wiley.

Stanovich, K.E. (1986) "Matthew effects in reading: Some consequences of individual differences in the acquisition of literacy." *Reading Research Quarterly 21*, 4, 360–407.

Stanovich, K.E., Siegel, L.S., and Gottardo, A. (1997) "Converging evidence for phonological and surface subtypes of reading disability." *Journal of Educational Psychology 89*, 1, 114–127.

Stanovich, K.E., West, R.F., and Cunningham, A.E. (1991) "Beyond phonological processes: Print exposure and orthographic processing." In S.A. Brady and D.P. Shankweiler (eds) *Phonological Processes in Literacy: A Tribute to Isabelle Y. Liberman*, pp. 219–235. Hillsdale, NJ: Lawrence Erlbaum Associates, Inc.

Stuart, M. and Howard, D. (1995) "KJ: A developmental deep dyslexic." *Cognitive Neuropsychology 12*, 8, 793–824.

Tallal, P., Miller, S., and Fitch, R. (1993) "Neurobiological basis of speech: A case for the preeminence of temporal processing." *Annals of the New York Academy of Sciences 682*, 27–47.

Tanguay, P.B. (2002) *Nonverbal Learning Disabilities at School.* Philadelphia: Jessica Kingsley Publishers.

Thompson, S. (1997) *The Source for Nonverbal Learning Disorders.* East Moline, IL: LinguiSystems.

Willcut, E.G. and Gaffney-Brown, R. (2004) "Etiology of dyslexia, ADHD, and related difficulties: Using genetic methods to understand comorbidity." *Perspectives 30*, Spring, 12–15.

Wolf, M. (1991) "Naming speed and reading: The contribution of the cognitive neurosciences." *Reading Research Quarterly 25*, 2, 123–141.

Wolf, M. and Bowers, P.G. (1999) "The double-deficit hypothesis for the developmental dyslexia." *Journal of Educational Psychology 91*, 3, 415–438.

ABOUT THE AUTHOR

Alan M. Hultquist, Ed.D. is a licensed school psychologist. He currently lives in the US with his husband of more than 20 years. He has both a Bachelor's degree and a Master's degree in special education as well as a Doctor's degree in educational psychology. He has worked professionally in the fields of special education and psychology since 1979. His articles have appeared in *Annals of Dyslexia, Journal of Psychoeducational Assessment,* and *Journal of Emotional and Behavioral Disorders.*

INDEX